English in Brief

A Course in Summary Writing

Alan Proud

Edward Arnold

First published 1977 by
Edward Arnold (Publishers) Ltd
25 Hill Street, London W1X 8LL

British Library Cataloguing in Publication Data

Proud, Alan
    English in brief.
    1. English language - Composition and exercises
    I. Title
    428' .2   PE1477

    ISBN 0-7131-0157-1

Set IBM by 𝓕 Tek Art, Croydon, Surrey.

Printed in Great Britain by Unwin Bros Ltd,
The Gresham Press, London and Old Woking.

Contents

To the Teacher

English in Brief is a carefully graded course which aims to give a thorough grounding in the skills of précis-writing and summarising. Too often students are expected to tackle summarising with very little practice — to take a great leap in a few weeks from not doing this kind of English to writing quite lengthy summaries. This book avoids this sink or swim approach by starting from first principles and gradually introducing the reader to the range of skills needed. Work starts with sentences and builds up slowly through paragraphs to full-length summaries of the kind found in external exams. The book is designed to be used over a two-year period beginning in the fourth year but it could equally well be used for a more concentrated course in the fifth year at school or the first year of Further Education.

The early sections of *English in Brief* concentrate on instilling the essential skills of précis-writing — in the belief that these are basic to all summarising — but the book also places considerable emphasis on the less formal aspects of this important sector of English work. There are numerous exercises involving selective summary of the types now set in many examinations and attention is also given to the abstracting of information presented in graph and statistical form.

The passages on which the book is based have been chosen both for their suitability as summary material and for their likely appeal to young people. While the primary purpose is to assist students in the necessary business of gaining exam certificates, the wider aim is to stimulate interest and increase attainment in an activity which is of great importance in adult life.

A.P.

Acknowledgements

The Publisher's thanks are due to the following for permission to reproduce copyright material:

Jonathan Cape Ltd for an extract from J.G. Ballard's *The Drought*; Penguin Books Ltd and contributors for extracts from *The School That I'd Like*, ed. Edward Blishen (1969); J.M. Dent & Sons Ltd for an extract from Arthur Bourne's *Pollute and Be Damned*; A.D. Peters & Co. Ltd for an extract from Ray Bradbury's *The Silver Locusts*; Weidenfeld & Nicholson Ltd for an extract from *Nature in the Round*, ed. Nigel Calder; Chatto & Windus Ltd for extracts from R. Carrington's *Elephants* and *A Biography of the Sea*; The Bodley Head for an extract from Charles Chaplin's *My Autobiography*; Hodder & Stoughton Ltd for extracts from Peter Scott's *The Eye of the Wind*, Colin Cross's *Adolf Hitler* and A.R. van der Loeff's *Avalanche*; 'Grim Stories from the Titanic's Survivors' appeared in the now defunct 'Daily Herald'; McIntosh and Otis Inc. for an excerpt from Beryl Williams' and Samuel Epstein's *The Great Houdini*; A.D. Peters for an extract from C.S. Forester's *Death to the French*; Curtis Brown Ltd, London on behalf of the Estate of Sir Philip Gibbs for an extract from *The Pageant of the Years*; Leslie Frewin Books Ltd for an extract from P. Goldring's *The Broiler-House Society*; Maurice Temple Smith Ltd for an extract from Gerald Haigh's *The Reluctant Adolescent*; Mrs E.W. Hildick for an extract from *A Close Look at Magazines and Comics*; Curtis Brown Ltd for an extract from James Leasor's *The Plague and the Fire*; Priory Press Ltd for an extract from A.R.K. Mitchell's *Drugs — the Parents' Dilemma*; Mr George Perry for a passage for précis, 'Critical Analysis' (GCE Examination Paper, Associated Board); Michael Joseph Ltd for an extract from 'Miss Read''s *News from Thrush Green*; Martin Secker & Warburg Ltd for an extract from Piers Paul Read's

Alive!: Story of the Andes Survivors; Vera Ryder and Robert Hale Ltd for an extract from *The Little Victims Play*; Routledge & Kegan Paul Ltd for an extract from M.W. Thring's *Man, Machines and Tomorrow*; The Hamlyn Group for an extract from F. Wilkinson's *Guns*; the 'Daily Telegraph' for an extract from Diana Winsor's 'Now Shake dem Bones'; David Higham Ltd for an extract from John Wyndham's *Chocky* and Oxford University Press for an extract from Taya Zinkin's *India*.

Short extracts from the following books are also included:

The Tombs of Atuan by Ursula Le Guin (Gollancz); *Your Body* by D.S. Daniell (Willis & Hepworth); *We Are Not Alone* by W. Sullivan (Hodder & Stoughton); *Send Down a Dove* by C. MacHardy (Wm. Collins); *Book of the British Countryside* (AA Drive Publications); *Animal Facts and Fallacies* by O.P. Breland (Faber & Faber); *The Moon of Gomrath* by A. Garner (Wm. Collins); *Book of the Seaside* (AA Drive Publications); *The Story of Jodrell Bank* by R. Piper (Hutchinson); *The 15 Wonders of the World* (Gollancz); *Dogs* by Wendy Borer (Hamlyn Books); *The Hobbit* by J.R.R. Tolkien (Allen and Unwin); *Penguin Car Handbook* by R. Ireson (Penguin); *Supernature* by Lyall Watson (Hodder and Stoughton); *Voyages of Captain Cook* by Chris Lloyd (Cresset Press); *A Town Like Alice* by N. Shute (Heinemann); *The Sixth Wife* by Jean Plaidy (Hale); *New Lives, New Landscapes* by N. Fairbrother (Architectural Press); *The Black Boxer* by H.E. Bates (Jonathan Cape); *Birds, Beasts and Relatives* by G. Durrell (Collins); *The Blazing South West* by P.I. Wellman (Foulsham); *The Pearl* by J. Steinbeck (Heinemann); *Consumers' Guide to the Protection of the Environment* by J. Holliman (Ballantine); *The Intercom Conspiracy* by Eric Ambler (Weidenfeld), 'Yellow Trail from Texas' by Tim Slessor ('The Listener') and *Companion Guide to Coast of NE England* by J. Seymour (Wm Collins).

1

Introductory

Young people are often critical of the type of work set in English lessons during their final years at school. "What is the point of Creative Writing?" they object. "I will never put pen to paper again in this way when I leave school." Answering endless comprehension questions must often seem an irrelevant waste of time, too. But one kind of English which *is* of practical value to many people in their working lives is summarising and it is advice and practice in that activity that this book aims to provide.

Everyone, of course, summarises in the normal course of events but we don't usually commit our summaries to paper. If your mother asks you what you did last night ("Whatever kept you out so late?") or your friend wants an account of the new film at the local cinema then a summary is being requested. These oral reports come as second nature to us: our memory sifts through what we did or what we saw and we have no trouble in producing the shortened version. A similar informal process is at work when we write a letter to a friend or relative giving the latest news. There is obviously no need to include all the trivial routine details of what we had for lunch or whether we cleaned our teeth at night. We include only the important events which give significance to our lives and which will interest our reader.

When it comes to formal summarising on paper, a surprising number of men and women find this a valuable skill in their occupations. In the professions, the business world, the Civil Service, and in journalism, there is a clear need for the extraction of important data from the mass of reports and statistics which circulate. The ability to see through the trees to the wood is prized and rewarded. During the Second World War, Winston Churchill's frequent requests to his advisers for reports "on one sheet of paper" meant that summary-writing must have been one of the principal activities in the corridors (and air-raid shelters) of power.

One other obvious reason for students devoting time to the practice of summarising is that the exercise features in the English syllabus of most external examination Boards. This is because being able to write a summary is a good test of one's ability a) to understand what one reads; b) to distinguish between what is important and relevant and what is not; and c) to express ideas and information in a lucid, logical style. All these qualities are worth developing both because of the wider issues of personal development and career prospects and from the narrower viewpoint of success in exams. (And not only in English: think what an important part summarising plays in, say, History.)

Basically, what is needed in summary-writing is common sense but there are certain techniques, easily acquired through practice, which will enable you to approach this aspect of English with extra confidence.

As most readers of this book will be studying summarising for exam purposes rather than as an end in itself, it will be important to distinguish between two broad approaches which examiners adopt nowadays. The first involves the traditional discipline of précis-writing. *Précis* was originally a French word which has obvious connections with the English *precision* and *precise*. It requires the condensing of a piece of connected writing to about one third of its original length, the aim being to include only the essential facts or argument of the writer. There are some basic principles that one can learn on the way to becoming a competent précis-writer and these will be outlined at the beginning of Section 2 because they are relevant to the whole field of summarising.

The second, and currently the more widely-set, form of summarising is where examiners ask you to extract from a passage information which relates to only one or two stated objectives. For instance, you might be asked to study a survey drawn up by a consumer organisation on refrigerators and then to present their findings about a) value for money and b) after-sales service. You might also be required to consider sets of statistics and then have to write a report, not on the overall figures, but analysing particular trends that they show. There are many executives in industry, commerce and advertising who do this as a regular part of their job. The more expertise you can gain at this stage the better, because, once learnt, the principles will be with you for life — whether you are drawing up the annual Chairman's Report of a giant corporation or whether you're only telling your wife or your husband what a hard day you've had at the office.

2

Basic Principles of Summarising

A fundamental point to remember in all summary-writing is that you must never add anything of your own to the given passage. You may feel impelled to comment on what the writer says, especially if you disagree with him, but this impulse must be resisted. Your shortened version must, of necessity, be a pale reflection of the original. Your job is to convey the bare bones of someone else's brain-child.

Especially for examination purposes, you must endeavour to re-phrase in your own words what you select as essential. Only then can you demonstrate that you have understood what you have read. Remember that one of the aims of summary-writing in exams is to test your powers of comprehension. This necessity to re-phrase puts you at a disadvantage because the original writer had first choice of words and presumably used the most effective for his purpose. Your version will be second best but you are aiming at clarity and brevity, not at winning the 'style of the year' award. Of course, there are many terms and phrases which you cannot adequately translate into your own words and these may be retained. It would be pointless, for instance, to try to find synonyms for *Geography* or *politics* and long-winded alternatives would be inappropriate.

Précis Proper

Writing summaries of the traditional précis type, where one's primary aim is to give a shortened version of the original, is greatly simplified if one can follow certain guidelines. Practice in these is given later but it will be convenient to summarise them here.

i)   All précis is written in Reported Speech. This means that Direct Speech in quotation marks is never used, nor are the first person pronouns. Verbs are pushed back into the past because you are reporting what someone has already written.

ii) As only the main points are required, the following can be cut: lists, analogies (parallels), examples and repetition. Go for general words and principles.

iii) Be ruthless in pruning all description, figurative language, picturesque English, and all supporting quotations. Use only plain statements.

More detailed guidance will be found on pages 13-19.

Précis – Basic Technique

Bearing in mind the above pointers, then, how does one set about writing a précis? The following routine will ensure that you are on the right lines.

1 Read the passage to be summarised several times until you are quite sure what it is about.

2 Go slowly through it again making a note *in your own words* of each main point made by the writer. In general, it is best to retain the order in which these ideas or facts or opinions occur.

3 Now re-read the original for the last time and check that your list of main points has not omitted anything of importance.

4 Set aside the passage and use your notes as the basis for a first rough draft of your summary. Be sure to write in proper connected English.

5 Count the words you have used and see whether the total lies within the limit set. If it is easily within then you have probably missed out something important so go back and check through the original once again. If it is too long then work through it, cutting by crossing out what is not essential, or re-phrasing in a more economical way.

6 Make a last word count and then copy out your final version. At the end, state the number of words you have used.

This six-point plan is valid for all précis work, whatever the length of material to be condensed and whatever limits of space one may have. Exam candidates, however, should bear in mind these additional suggestions. Leave a gap between your fair copy and your preliminary work, which you should cancel with a single diagonal line. This helps the examiner to know where to begin marking and he may well give you credit for systematic notes even if your final summary is below standard, or, if you run out of time, unfinished. Be honest, too, in your statement of the total of words used. Don't put "120" if you've written 150. You will be penalised for exceeding the limit anyway and trying to disguise woolly writing by attempting to pull the wool over the examiner's eyes will only make things worse.

Selective Summarising

So far we have concentrated on the sort of summary where a précis of all the original is required. Now we turn to the more flexible summarising which involves extracting only certain information. This is the type of summary that is now set by the majority of the exam. Boards and it is an activity in which most of us will be involved sooner or later in "real life".

In its most straightforward form this type of summarising may be an extension of the questions set on a passage for comprehension. You may be asked, for example, to say what impression you have formed from the extract of a character or place involved, and the limit of words to be used may be 60 or so. You might also be asked to isolate and reproduce any element of fact or opinion which occurs among other related or unrelated material.

In its most elaborate form, this selective summarising often involves a separate extract of its own, or a series of shorter pieces, sometimes of comment or opinion, and you are asked to write a stated number of paragraphs of controlled length — perhaps 150 words in all. Here again, you must read the given material several times to establish its general meaning. Then you will ascertain just which aspects of what you have read are involved in the summary. You then proceed to jot down in note form, using your own words as far as possible, the relevant information, which may be widely scattered. Next, as with a full-scale précis, you re-read the original to make sure you have omitted nothing of significance. Finally, you write out your paragraphs in clear, connected English, making sure they are within the stated limits. If they are too long, a quick pruning will be necessary.

Remember that in this less formal and, many would say, more realistic type of summary there is no need to use the rigid conventions of précis. Just give the required information in straightforward English using, for instance, whichever tense comes naturally.

Reference to the syllabus of your own exam. Board and to recent past or specimen papers will show you which type of summary to expect. All types will be found in this book. In Section 3 I have given some preliminary practice in the basic skills of précis-writing. The main part, Section 4, consists of a variety of material, graded in difficulty, leading up to work of external examination standard. If you work conscientiously through these sections you should be ready for your rendezvous with the examiners and, what is more, you will have acquired a fundamental skill of great use in your further education and in your working life.

3

Preliminaries

Direct and Reported Speech

When we quote the actual words of a speaker we use *Direct Speech*, e.g. "I think Liverpool will win the First Division," said Tony. The actual words that Tony said are quoted and, as a sign of this, they are enclosed in quotation marks (or, as some would call them, inverted commas, speech marks, or even 66s and 99s). If Tony's remark was being reported to someone else later it would be transposed into what we call, naturally enough, *Reported Speech*: Tony said he thought Liverpool would win the First Division.

As a general rule, all formal précis is written in Reported Speech and when writing about what someone else said or did, you would adopt this style. This need cause no problems if you follow certain guidelines, most of which can be deduced from the following examples:

Direct Speech	Reported Speech
"We can't go on seeing each other like this," she said.	She said that they couldn't go on seeing each other like that.
"I want you to understand, here and now," declared the new teacher, "that I will stand no nonsense."	The new teacher declared that he wanted them to understand, there and then, that he would stand no nonsense.
"Drop that gun, Sam, or you're a dead man," ordered the cop.	The cop ordered Sam to drop the gun or he would be a dead man.

"I watched TV for about three hours last night," said Joyce.	Joyce said that she had watched TV for about three hours the previous night.
"I watch about three hours' TV every night," remarked Joyce.	Joyce remarked that she watches about three hours' TV every night.

It will be seen that in Reported Speech: i) the quotation marks disappear; ii) that 1st and 2nd person pronouns I/me, we/us, you, are put into the 3rd person he/she, him/her, they/them; iii) if the sense demands it, present tense verbs are put into the past and iv) words of immediacy such as here, now and this are replaced by more remote terms such as there, then and that.

One cannot rigidly lay down rules which apply to every passage for précis: you must apply your common sense and adopt the style which best suits the subject. In general, however, and especially in exams of the "Reduce this extract to 120 words" variety, it often helps to begin with a formula such as "The writer says that . . ." or "X writes that . . ." In this way you will naturally fall into the right format.

Keeping It Simple

All the statements printed in this section are written in an inflated or long-winded style. Each can be written more simply and economically. See how briefly you can summarise them, retaining essential information only. They can be adequately re-phrased in the number of words shown in brackets. Can you beat these targets?

1 Taking your own life is against the law. (3)
2 Our expectation was hopefully to meet up with some people we were acquainted with. (6)
3 Consequent upon the lack of rainfall, potatoes, turnips, carrots, parsnips and beetroot have been in short supply. (8)
4 "I swear", he cried, "by the sun, and by the blue sky of heaven, and by the fire of love that burns my heart, that if you grant my prayer, while they exist you shall never behold me again." (18)
5 The two objects were not dissimilar but while one was the real thing, the other was an imitation closely resembling the original. (14)

6   I have a great aversion to people who pretend to be what they are not. (3)

7   One dress was in the style of a bygone era but the other could have come straight from the workrooms of the French capital. (13)

8   The man who presented the programme of recorded pop-music on the radio was born on the other side of the Atlantic but he had lived within a stone's throw of Big Ben since the termination of hostilities after the Second World War. (14)

9   The tables of facts and figures made available to all those entitled to vote proved beyond a shadow of a doubt that the party which was in power had not succeeded in putting into practice what it had promised to do when it last went to the country. (18)

10 Instead of post-primary educational establishments for the 11-16 age group being made up of those which catered for academic children and those which enrolled the non-academic, the trend during recent years has been to set up institutions which are attended by pupils of all abilities. (18)

Figurative Language

In précis and summary writing you must seek out the facts. Never mind how picturesque or evocative is the language in which they are expressed. Re-write these sentences in plain English, replacing all figurative expressions with straightforward literal statements.

1   The school was a hive of industry: the classrooms buzzed with the noise of eager pupils going about their activities like worker bees gathering information, experience and house points.

2   "Friends, Romans, countrymen, lend me your ears," pleaded Antony, as he addressed the assembled mob.

3   Councillor Cliché declared that he could sit on the fence no longer but would explore every avenue and leave no stone unturned in an endeavour to prevent the escalation of expenditure.

4   Apathy has been described as a cancer which can sap the strength of a democracy, leaving it vulnerable to the virus of Communism.

5   The winger darted down the flank torturing the defence before slotting an inch-perfect cross to the striker who hammered it home.

6   The shout rebounded, reverberated, re-echoed endlessly through the vast canyon, a veritable cathedral of nature, a monument of majestic might.

7   The news that Dawn Delight, the face that launched a thousand films, was to retire hit the entertainment world like a bombshell.

8   As soon as the doors of the store were opened, the bargain-hunters charged in like a herd of frenzied steers who had scented water after a long trek through the desert.

9   The group played as if possessed, drowning the hall in an ocean of sound; wave after wave of amplified chords battered the ears of the fervent fans.

10   The odour of roast pork sets my taste-buds tingling and my nostrils quivering as no other smell on earth: I can hardly wait to sink my teeth into the sweet, crisp crackling.

Lists and Examples

There is no place in précis and summaries for lists and examples. What you must do is to give the broad outline only and cut all detail. Re-write the sentences that follow, replacing all lists and examples by shorter expressions.

1   The new delivery of exercise books, folders and file-paper was put in the stockroom.

2   About fifty lorries, buses, vans and cars were destroyed in the blaze.

3   Composers such as Mozart, Haydn and Beethoven and writers like Shakespeare, Dickens and Balzac are geniuses whose lives conform to no accepted patterns.

4   When we went abroad we stored all our chairs, tables, settees, carpets, curtains, beds, bedding, crockery and cutlery in a warehouse.

5   I am no good at sprinting, hurdling, middle or long-distance running: I am better at discus, javelin and shot.

6   The delegate representing Great Britain, Ireland, France, Germany, Belgium, Holland, Italy, Denmark and Luxembourg voted against the measure.

7   He is a man who mends pipes, instals baths and wash-basins — everything, in fact, including the kitchen sink.

8   Twentieth-century man is subject to far more pressures — emotional, financial, social and environmental — than were his ancestors in previous ages.

9   The farmer sold his cows, horses, sheep and pigs and went

over to wheat, barley and oats.

10 The town has acres of sub-standard housing, crowded tenements and dilapidated Victorian terraces. The planners hope to move the men, women and children who live there to an area with pleasant shopping-centres, parks, sports grounds and recreational facilities.

Paraphrasing

One valuable skill which is associated with summarising is the ability to put into your own words what you have selected as important in the original. The primary skill, one could say, lies in choosing the important facts, but almost as vital is the secondary skill of re-stating these facts in language of your own. In doing this, you demonstrate that you have assimilated what you have read. This ability to re-word is called *paraphrasing* and in this section you will be able to try your hand at it.

With the statements that follow, all you have to do is to put them into your own words. There is no need to reduce the number of words. Imagine that these are the selected main points which you are going to incorporate in a summary: the difficulty lies in devising acceptable alternative versions. Bear in mind that some key words and technical terms cannot be replaced satisfactorily and may be retained (e.g. industry, in sentence no. 1; banks, no. 7; vampire, no. 11).

1   The chief object of industry in this country is to make profits.
2   Homework could be abolished if children were made to raise their productivity during the school day.
3   A splendid procession of lords and ladies in flowing robes preceded the Queen who looked neither to the left nor to the right.
4   Young people have far too much money in their pockets and they lack the experience to spend it wisely.
5   Climate has a great influence on cities both in the way that they are built and in the way their inhabitants organise their lives.
6   Some people find that music is an aid to concentration when studying but others feel that it is a distraction.
7   In order to finance their activities, terrorist organisations often resort to armed raids on banks.
8   Educating boys and girls together is sensible; the social

advantages outweigh any possible erosion in standards of attainment.

9　The benefits of living in the country are obvious in the summer but there is a lot to be said for city life in the winter.

10　At the rate we are going, the United Kingdom will not be united for much longer.

11　A scream of anguish rose from the coffin as the stake was driven through the vampire's heart.

12　It is no good looking back nostalgically to the time when one could buy a fish and a penn'orth of chips and still have change from sixpence — those days have gone for ever.

Critical Analysis

Criticise these attempts at paraphrasing the sentences in the previous section.

1　The main aim of industry in Britain is to raise capital.

2　To higher productivity during schooldays, homework could be abolished.

3　The important-looking Queen was followed by a procession of well-dressed gentries.

4　Juveniles today do not deserve the large amount of money they are given as they do not know how to spend it correctly.

5　The construction of a large community both physically and mentally is done in accordance with the weather.

6　Music when working can either be a help or a hindrance.

7　Terrorist organisations have nothing better to do than hold up banks.

8　Co-education is better because although there have been queries on the difference of intelligence between the two groups, more advantages have shown on the social aspect.

9　The country in summer is really lovely and warm but the winter is very cold and miserable in the towns.

10　If Great Britain keep going in their present direction, they will eventually become un-united.

11　The vampire's screams could be heard rising from its deathbed as the steak was driven through its heart.

12　In the olden days you could by fish and chips and still have change of sixpence but nowadays the sixpence bearly exists.

Sentences to Simplify

Bearing in mind the points made in previous sections, write a summary of each of the following sentences as briefly and simply as you can. Avoid copying the original language and, where necessary, use Reported Speech.

1   "I think that people who go in for fox-hunting, hare-coursing, cock-fighting and pheasant-shooting should be put behind bars," declared Tony.

2   Life is a game where a small minority of players bend the rules and prosper but by and large the great majority are good sports and play it straight.

3   The rain came down in buckets so we had to spend our time playing cards, chess, draughts, Scrabble, Ludo and Monopoly.

4   "If you are desirous of incurring some permanent re-arrangement of your physiognomy you are adopting the correct tactical approach to the problem," remarked the gentleman whose own nasal structure could no longer be described as aquiline.

5   The study of the sun, the moon, the planets and the stars is a serious one but the belief that the position of the stars can influence human affairs is hardly scientific.

6   "I'll see you back here in an hour," said Mrs Walton to her husband. "I've got to call at the butcher's, the baker's, the greengrocer's and the fishmonger's."

7   If one takes immediate corrective action as soon as the first signs of any damage or malfunction appear, then one can obviate the eventual need for major refurbishment.

8   The fiery sun shone down relentlessly day after day like an evil eye scorching the grass, withering the trees, drying up the streams, the rivers, the ponds and lakes until the whole land cracked and crumbled into despairing dust.

9   "Get ye gone, ye men of Gath — each unto his own home!" cried the herald. "The Angel of Death hath smitten the hosts and the mighty men of battle are no more!"

10   Those who indulge in perpetual peregrinations will never attain a state of financial stability.

11   The movement for the emancipation of the female of the species has progressed by leaps and bounds of late and recent legislation has put another nail in the coffin of male dominance.

12   Reducing a piece of writing to its essentials is greatly facilitated if one has a good store of words at one's command.

One-sentence Summaries

It is unlikely that you will be able to write a satisfactory summary if you do not understand the meaning of the original — summarising is first of all a test of comprehension. One thing to remember in this connection is that the number of words used in making a statement is no indication of its importance. A statement made in 30 words is not necessarily more significant than one made in three. "Danger: unexploded bomb" carries at least as much impact as the more grandiose "In the interests of hygiene, customers are kindly requested to refrain from smoking within the area of the Food Hall."

One of the valuable side-effects of a thorough grounding in précis techniques is the ability to see through a mass of words to the essential core of meaning. This comes with experience but a valuable preliminary exercise is having to express in just one sentence the basic "message" contained in a whole paragraph. This is the requirement in the pieces that follow: read each paragraph carefully then summarise its contents in one sentence only. Some of the paragraphs are taken from fiction and you will be able to discard purely descriptive details and figurative language. The remainder are from non-fiction sources where the emphasis is already on the factual and you will have to concentrate on conveying the main line of thought, cutting all side-issues, examples and supporting material.

i)   In the deep valley, in the twilight, the apple trees were on the eve of blossoming; here and there among the shadowed boughs one flower had opened early, rose and white, like a faint star. Down the orchard aisles, in the thick, new, wet grass, the little girl ran for the joy of running; hearing the call she did not come at once, but made a long circle before she turned her face towards home. The mother waiting in the doorway of the hut, with the firelight behind her, watched the tiny figure running and bobbing like a bit of thistledown blown over the darkening grass beneath the trees.

ii)   When you want to move any part of your body, your brain sends an order down the motor nerves, which connect with the muscles which operate the joints. Every movement you wish to make is ordered by your brain; whether it be to turn your neck, move any of your limbs, open your mouth or twitch your nose. If you decide to move a chair towards you and sit down, your brain sends a series of messages down the appropriate motor nerves to your shoulders, elbows, hands and fingers to move the chair, and to your knees, feet, back and other limbs to sit down. These messages are passed so quickly that it all seems instantaneous.

iii)   Ours is a wonderful world. Of all the planets in the solar system it seems to be the only one on which life, as we know it, could survive. Mars is too dry and its air is apparently so poor in oxygen that the astronauts who land there will be unable to build fires. Venus seems far too hot. Mercury has no day-night cycle, keeping the same torrid side continuously facing the sun. The outer planets have hydrogen-dominated, frigid atmospheres in which the higher forms of earth life could not exist.

iv)   Moore swayed and grabbed the back of the helmsman's chair to steady himself as the submarine began to roll more heavily on her new course. Regaining his balance he straightened up and removed his tobacco tin from his top pocket. He opened the tin and fished out a paper spilling a little tobacco into it. With a quick, practised, darting movement of his tongue he licked the gummed side of the paper and rolled it into a neat tube. The straggly ends, where the strands of tobacco pushed out, he nipped off with his finger and thumb and dropped them back carefully into the tin. The flick of his lighter briefly illuminated his dark, gipsy-like features in the dim red glow of the control-room.

v)   That part of the earth's crust called the British Isles seems eternal and unchanging in its shape. But this is only when it is viewed against the time-scale of human history, which measures time in hundreds or at the most thousands of years. Viewed against a geological time-scale, where the years are measured in their thousands of millions, the surface of Britain has been in continual movement: folding, twisting, collapsing, erupting and heaving itself above and below the sea under the stresses set up in the bowels of the earth.

vi)   Probably more people are killed in India by snakes than in any other country. Some authorities estimate that approximately 20,000 deaths from snake bite occur in India each year, but others believe that this estimate is too high. This relatively high death rate is probably the result of the natives' habit of going barelegged and barefooted, and of the fact that in some areas snakes are not habitually killed. In the United States, it is thought that between 1,500 to 1,800 people are bitten each year. Of reported cases, only about five per cent are fatal, so that about 100 snake bite deaths annually would be a fair estimate.

vii)   They were a small people, not more than four feet high, deep-chested, with narrow waists, and long, slender arms and legs. They wore short tunics, belted and sleeveless, and their feet were bare. Some had cloaks of white eagle feathers, though these were marks of rank rather than a protection. They carried deeply curved bows, and from their belts hung on one side quivers of white arrows, and on the other broad stabbing swords. Each rode a small white horse, and some sat proudly erect, though most drooped over the pommels of their saddles, and a few lay irrevocably still across their horses' necks, and the reins were held by others. All together they numbered close on five hundred.

viii)   Humans, like many animals, love lolling about in the sun. The lazy lion — such an expert hunter that he has nothing to do for much of his day — dozes and rolls in the sunshine for the pure joy of it. *Homo sapiens*, with far less time to spare, takes it more seriously. Rank upon rank of people lie flat on their stomachs or backs along the beaches of Britain, roasting in the sunshine with relentless determination. The object is to acquire an even, healthy looking brown called a sun-tan.

ix)   Russia sent up the first artificial satellite on 4th October, 1957, and although there was no man aboard, or even an animal, the event caused a tremendous sensation. It was, after all, the first object to be thrown beyond the earth's atmosphere which did not at once return to earth — and it was circling the earth once every one and a half hours, at a height of some five hundred and sixty miles and at the tremendous speed of more than eighteen thousand miles per hour, and sending out radio messages at the same time. Nor was this all. The Sputnik contained instruments and a radio transmitter. These instruments were sensitive to light and heat, and they altered the wave-length and rhythm of the Sputnik's radio signals whenever conditions changed inside the satellite.

x)   The Prince of Wales, the future Edward VII, had the honour on November 4th, 1890, of inaugurating the first electrically operated tube railway in the world. Accompanied by his elder son, Albert, Duke of Clarence, and leading scientists and engineers, the Prince went down to King William Street Station in a richly upholstered lift. On the platform, in the presence of the Lord Mayor, the Aldermen and the Sheriff of the City of London, he was given a golden key, and with it he operated an illuminated switch which lit up the royal party as well as supplying current to the rails. The train then left for Stockwell on the south bank of the Thames, where a traditional banquet was served in honour of electricity, the tube and the Victorian age generally.

xi)   Rifleman Matthew Dodd went on up the hill. As soon as he was safe from immediate pursuit he sat down in the cover of a whin-bush to reload his rifle — reloading took so long that it was always advisable to do it in the first available moment of leisure, lest one should encounter danger calling for instant use of the rifle. He took a cartridge from his pouch and bit the bullet — a half-inch sphere of lead — out of the paper container. He poured the powder into the barrel, all save a pinch which went into the priming pan, whose cover he carefully replaced. He folded the empty cartridge into a wad, which he pushed down the barrel on top of the charge with the ramrod which he took from its socket along the barrel. Then he spat the bullet into the muzzle; it only fell down an inch or so, for it happened to be one of the more tightly-fitting bullets — extreme precision of manufacture was not demanded or considered necessary by those in authority. Since he could not coax the bullet down the rifling, he reached behind him to where a little mallet hung from his belt by a string through a hole in the handle. The fact that Dodd carried one of these tools proved that he was one of the careful ones of his regiment — it was not a service issue. Standing the rifle up on its butt he rested the ramrod on the bullet and tapped sharply with the mallet; musket and ramrod were so long that only a tall man could do this easily. The blows of the mallet drove the bullet down the rifling until at last it rested safely on top of the wadding; then Dodd hung the mallet on his belt again and replaced the ramrod in its groove. After that he had only to make sure that the flint was in good condition, and then his rifle was ready to fire again.

xii)   Kippering is a simple process. The fish are split down the back (Messrs L. Robson and Son have a German machine which does this job and replaces an army of fisher girls), soaked in brine for twenty minutes, then hung on tenter hooks (hence the expression) which are just bent nails in sticks about five feet long, and the tenter sticks are then hung on the racks inside the kiln. The kilns are very tall, and if a kiln is to be filled men clamber up the racks and then, perched there precariously, pass the loaded tenter sticks up from man to man — the topmost man putting them on the racks. Then a smouldering fire of sawdust and chips (always supposed to be oak, but many curers like a little soft-wood mixed with it) is lit on the floor of the kiln and is kept going for from fourteen to twenty hours.

More Paragraphs

Not all paragraphs can be satisfactorily reduced to one sentence — although, of course, we can summarise even a whole book in a few words if we want only the most general outline of its contents or theme. When, however, we want to give someone a fair idea of what a paragraph is about, this can usually be done in roughly one third of the original length.

We can begin now to follow the plan that applies to all formal précis-writing where a summary of the whole is required. Having read the original and, we hope, understood it, we note down in our own words the main points that the writer makes in the order that he makes them. He may make only one, followed by supporting material, or he may introduce several new ideas in the space of one paragraph. In either case, remember to demonstrate that you have taken in the original by putting into words of your own the important ideas encountered.

In the pieces that follow, read each one carefully and then make notes of the main points. In the ordinary way these would then be linked to make your summary but in order to emphasise the importance of this stage, all you are asked to do this time is to list the main points. It will be interesting to compare your list with others in your group. Remember that although the wording may be different, the essential facts should be the same.

i)   Alsatians, Labrador Retrievers, Collies and Boxers are all used as guide dogs, though Alsatians are in the great majority. A guide dog must not be aggressive, suspicious or nervous, and must have initiative and a willingness to work. Only bitches are used because they are generally temperamentally more suitable than males. Guide dogs are accepted between the ages of ten months and three years and their training lasts four months. As well as simple obedience training, the bitch must learn to allow for the width and height of the person she is leading when going round obstacles. Traffic training consists of teaching the dog to understand that if a moving vehicle is within a certain area she must stop or deliberately disobey the command "Forward", until the vehicle has either passed or is stationary. After the initial training period, the guide dog is introduced to her blind owner, and the two spend a further four weeks at the centre, training together. The average working life of a guide dog is about eight years.

ii)   I suppose hobbits need some description nowadays, since they have become rare and shy of the Big People, as they call us. They are (or were) a little people, about half our height, and smaller than the bearded Dwarves. Hobbits have no beards. There is little or no magic about them, except the ordinary everyday sort which helps them to disappear quietly and quickly when large stupid folk like you and me come blundering along, making a noise like elephants which they can hear a mile off. They are inclined to be fat in the stomach; they dress in bright colours (chiefly green and yellow); wear no shoes, because their feet grow natural leathery soles and thick warm brown hair like the stuff on their heads (which is curly); have long clever brown fingers, good-natured faces, and laugh deep fruity laughs (especially after dinner, which they have twice a day when they can get it). Now you know enough to go on with.

iii)   For the motorist whose journeys are short and numerous, or whose car remains in the garage for long periods, some independent means of charging the battery is very desirable. In winter, especially, a number of engine-starts may drain the battery beyond the stage at which the car dynamo can re-charge it in the subsequent running time. A simple way of overcoming this is by the use of a *trickle charger*; as its name implies, this is a device for feeding current to the battery at a low rate, or "trickle", and it almost always utilizes a transformer and metal rectifier to convert the alternating mains voltage to a direct voltage suitable to the battery. A typical charger includes an ammeter to indicate the charging current and a switch to select the appropriate output voltage to feed either a 6 volt or a 12 volt battery at a charging current of about 2 amperes, which is automatically reduced as the battery regains its charge. If the battery is working under particularly arduous conditions a low-rate trickle charger may be inadequate and a more elaborate charger capable of giving up to 5 amperes is advised. A home charger is intended for mounting on the garage wall and is normally connected to the battery terminals by a pair of leads with crocodile-type clips. On some cars a twin socket is permanently fitted to the facia panel to take either a charging plug or inspection lamp.

iv)   The classical method of water divining, or dowsing, is to cut a forked twig from a shade tree such as willow, hazel, or peach and to hold it out in front of the body parallel to the ground. In this position the muscles of the arm are under some tension; it is claimed that as the dowser approaches water, this tension somehow extends into the twig and induces it to move. The patterns of movement depend very much on the individual. Some say that an upward thrust of the dowsing rod indicates the upstream side of a water flow and the pattern of gyration indicates depth, but others disagree completely. There is a tremendous variation in technique among dowsers. Instruments in use include metal rods, coat hangers, whale-bone, copper wire, walking sticks, pitchforks, bakelite strips, surgical scissors, pendulums, and even, it is said, a German sausage. For each dowsing aid there are as many different ways of holding it and interpreting the way it moves. Just one thing takes all this extraordinary pantomime out of the area of sheer farce — the dowsers enjoy a very high rate of success.

v)   From the Journals of Captain Cook — January 6th 1779. At daybreak on the 16th, seeing the appearance of a bay, I sent Mr Bligh, with a boat from each ship, to examine it, being at this time three leagues off. Canoes now began to arrive from all parts; so that before ten o'clock there were not fewer than a thousand about the two ships, most of them crowded with people, and well laden with hogs and other productions of the island. We had the most satisfying proof of their friendly intentions; for we did not see a single person who had with him a weapon of any sort. Trade and curiosity alone had brought them off. Among such numbers as we had, at times, on board, it is no wonder that some should betray a thievish disposition. One of our visitors took out of the ship a boat's rudder. He was discovered; but too late to recover it. I thought this a good opportunity to show these people the use of firearms; and two or three muskets, and as many four-pounders, were fired over the canoe, which carried off the rudder. As it was not intended that any of the shot should take effect, the surrounding multitude of natives seemed rather more surprised than frightened.

vi)   And then it happened. In the middle of the night. Just below the top of the Kuhelihorn a great mass of snow broke loose with a crash like an explosion. Slowly it began to shift, it seemed to hesitate, but only for a little. A few seconds later the avalanche hurtled down, its path growing wider and wider, the force of the air driven before it blasting the village even before the thundering mass leapt upon the snow-covered houses and sheds like a wild beast. It lasted a far shorter time than anyone could have believed. One moment the village was safe and sound and fast asleep. The next, a great hole was torn in it. Part of it was still buried so deep in snow and wrapped in such deceptive silence that an onlooker would never have guessed the terrible thing that had happened. But part of it, even beyond the path of the avalanche, had houses blown down by blast, walls swept away, shutters and window frames ripped off and smashed. In an instant gaping black holes had been gashed in the white village and a white shroud of snow spread over its heart, just where Mr Baumgarten's office, the baker's shop and Gurtnelli's café stood clustered round the pump. The shattering blow which made everything that could split, burst, crack or smash fly to pieces with terrific force was followed by a minute or two of sinister silence. Then voices began to call. A woman screamed, one or two children cried, men's voices sounded harshly near at hand and further away. The alarm bell began to ring — a menacing sound above the stricken village.

vii)   Perhaps the greatest appeal of gliding is the simplicity of its basic concepts. In a glider you are competing against gravity. When you are going up you are winning, when you are coming down you are losing. There is something satisfyingly direct about it. As the glider is always sinking, the pilot's skill is in finding air which is rising faster. In the early days the easiest up-going air to find was the wind hitting a hill face and being deflected upwards. The glider's scope is limited by the length of the hill and the height of 1,000 or 2,000 feet to which the updraught extends. But the time a glider can fly in hill lift is limited only by the pilot's endurance. It becomes comparable with pole-squatting. With the exception of the five-hour requirement for the Silver C badge, duration is no longer a measure of gliding prowess. The discovery that thermal up-currents could be used opened up a whole new field of long-distance flying. By finding thermals — the bubbles of hot air which rise from some part of the ground that has become hotter in the sun than its surroundings — and circling tightly in the upgoing column, the glider gains enough height to set off in search of the next thermal, and so on across country until the sun gets too low to set off any more of them. The little white bun-shaped *cumulus* clouds of a summer's day are the tops of these thermals, and the pilot goes from cloud to cloud knowing, if the day is good, that there will be lift under each. In this country the record distance is 360 miles, and the world record — flown in the United States — is 550.

viii)   That perpetual servant of all work, the sun, had just risen, and begun to strike a light on the morning of the thirteenth of May, one thousand eight hundred and twenty-seven, when Mr Samuel Pickwick burst like another sun from his slumbers, threw open his chamber window, and looked out upon the world beneath. Goswell Street was at his feet, Goswell Street was on his right hand — as far as the eye could reach, Goswell Street extended on his left; and the opposite side of Goswell Street was over the way. "Such", thought Mr Pickwick, "are the narrow views of those philosophers who, content with examining the things that lie before them, look not to the truths which are hidden beyond. As well might I be content to gaze on Goswell Street for ever, without one effort to penetrate to the hidden countries which on every side surround it." And having given vent to this beautiful reflection, Mr Pickwick proceeded to put himself into his clothes, and his clothes into his portmanteau. Great men are seldom over-scrupulous in the arrangement of their attire; the operation of shaving, dressing, and coffee-imbibing was soon performed: and in another hour, Mr Pickwick, with his portmanteau in his hand, his telescope in his great-coat pocket, and his note-book in his waistcoat, ready for the reception of any discoveries worthy of being noted down, had arrived at the coach stand in St Martin's-le-Grand.

Statistics

One way of presenting factual information which is commonly used in industry, commerce and government is through graphs and statistics. Figures are precise in a way that words sometimes aren't and it is often clear and convenient to tabulate what one is trying to convey. You must learn to 'read' statistical tables and also to summarise in words all or part of the information that they contain. This section gives practice in such interpretation and selection. In all cases be sure to fulfil the precise requirements of the question. Just as in ordinary summarising you look for the main points, so, in this special kind, you will concentrate on picking out trends and general findings. You will not be able to include every figure given if you are to keep within the limit of words specified.

i)   This graph shows the number of people killed and seriously injured in road accidents in a large city during the years 1970-1976. In one short paragraph, summarise the information given about the numbers killed.

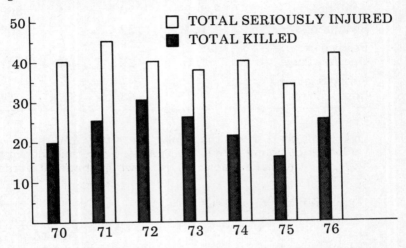

ii)   This table gives weather details for 7 seaside resorts on July 16th. Write a paragraph of about 60 words summarising the information presented.

	Hours of sun	Inches of rain	Max. temperature (F)
Scarborough	5	—	73
Margate	11	—	77
Hastings	3	—	66
Bournemouth	6	—	72
Torquay	3	—	70
Blackpool	1	.35	64
Aberdeen	4	.12	69

iii)   Various House Competitions are run in Fairside
Comprehensive School. Write a report in about 60 words of
this year's results, based on the following table of points
awarded.

	North House	South House	East House	West House
House Shield	3642	3780	3122	4013
Athletics	342	320	290	368
Swimming Gala	184	162	76	206
Festival of One Act Plays	26	28	36	22
Public Speaking Competition	31	33	31	14

iv)   This chart shows the results of a survey into the leisure
activities of young people in a small town during one winter
evening. Summarise the findings shown in about 90 words.

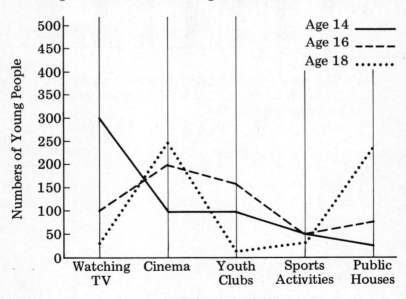

Summarising Speech

If you have forgotten the points to bear in mind when summarising passages that contain speech, turn back to page 13 and do some revision.

You may be faced with extracts which are mainly narrative but include speech; with transcripts of conversations; or with excerpts from plays which are wholly in dialogue form. A real life situation (as distinct from the various exam. tests) where the ability to summarise speech is vital, is when you have the job of producing minutes of a meeting, i.e. you have to give an accurate report of what was said by everyone taking part in the discussion. Obviously, you note down only the important points that are made so that after the meeting is over an official record of the substance of what was said will remain. Otherwise, memories of what transpired would have to be relied on and, as you will know from your own experience, different people's recollections of the same conversation can vary a great deal.

In the exercises that follow in this section, remember that your summaries will be written in reported speech. All quotation marks will disappear and so will question marks because you will re-phrase all direct questions and make them indirect. A useful formula here is to start the sentence with the speaker's name and use *if* or *whether* after the asking verb:

"Can you tell me the way to the stadium?" Val asked the traffic warden. (Direct Question)

Val asked the traffic warden if he could tell her the way to the stadium. (Indirect Question)

"Do you come here often?" Simon enquired of the blonde. (Direct)

Simon enquired of the blonde whether she came there often. (Indirect)

   i)   Write a report of this conversation in about 100 words.

"I think I'd like to join the army when I leave school, Mum," said Tony.

"Don't be silly," replied his Mum, "you'd never be able to get up in the morning."

"Be serious, Mum. I'd like an outdoor life with plenty of foreign travel."

"Northern Ireland's about as far as you'd get these days and I don't fancy . . ."

"That can't last for ever, " interrupted Tony. "Besides, they're more likely to send me to Germany, aren't they?"

His Dad looked up from his paper.

"I think you've left it too late, lad," he said. "In my day you could go to India, Egypt, Singapore — now we've nothing left."

"Don't start on again about how you won the war, Arthur," sighed Mrs Travis. "I think Tony would be much better off in a nice steady job in the Civil Service."

"No thanks — the excitement would kill me."

"Just you get through your exams," said his father "and then we'll see."

ii)   Write a summary of the following excerpt in no more than 100 words.

Suddenly, away in the distance, an owl hooted. Once. Twice. Three times. Then there was silence.

"Robin!" whispered Friar Tuck. "Wake up. Someone's coming."

In an instant Robin was wide-awake and buckling on his sword-belt.

"Where is Will?" he asked.

"Still out on the far side of the abbey," replied Tuck.

To the left could be heard the sound of horses and heavily armed men, the squeaking of carts and the groaning of timbers under strain.

"Take ten men and wait for me at the stunted oak," said Robin, his eyes already sparkling at the thought of a rich prize. "I am going to see what offerings the Normans have brought for us this time."

Followed by the remainder of the outlaws, Robin ghosted off into the shadows like some creature of the night, not a sound betraying where more than a score of men had vanished. It was as he had expected: his old adversary, the Sheriff of Nottingham, was sending another load of treasure to the safety of the abbey — bags of coin wrested in taxes, gold goblets and silver ornaments, richly worked bolts of cloth, casks of choicest wine.

"Right, lads," ordered Robin quietly as the carts lumbered by beneath their vantage point on the bracken-covered hill. "We'll take them at the stunted oak. We're in luck. The moon's just coming out from behind yon cloud."

iii)   The following is a transcript of part of a meeting of the School Council at Fairside Comprehensive. As secretary, write the minutes of the proceedings. There is no limit of words but include only the main outline of what was said.

Tom Reynolds:	As representative of 4F, I have been asked to raise the matter of a smoking-room for use at break and dinner-time.
Headmaster:	What do you mean, a smoking-room?
Tom Reynolds:	Well, sir, we all know that smoking goes on in the loos — I mean toilets, sir — and behind the bike-sheds and we thought it would be better to bring it out into the open.
Mrs Hurst:	I can't see how having a room would bring it into the open. I don't think the ladies on the staff would approve of a smoke-filled room. . .
Tom Reynolds:	You know what I mean. If all the smokers had a place to go and we had official permission to light up there, there'd be no need for all those sneaking patrols in the grounds at dinner-times.
Headmaster:	And which room did you have in mind?
Tom Reynolds:	Well, we hadn't really thought that far.
Jane Leggatt:	What about the empty room next to the stationery store?
Mr Jarrold:	No thanks. I don't want all my stock going up in flames. Besides, that's going to be Resources.
Tom Reynolds:	There'd be no danger, sir, if we had ash-trays and things. I know lots of the teachers smoke and the staffroom hasn't caught fire yet.
Headmaster:	I don't think that's a profitable line of argument, Reynolds. . .
Mrs Hurst:	Well I'm against the proposal on health grounds. It's common knowledge that smoking is bad for young people and I don't think we should encourage it.
Jane Leggatt:	But like Tom says, it happens anyway. Lots of girls in my form smoke and they're only thirteen.
Mr Jarrold:	What would the parents say — not to mention the local paper? I can see the headlines now: *Fags At Fairside*.
Tom Reynolds:	Well they have them at Eton, don't they?
Headmaster:	I think we're wandering from the point. What about having an area *in the grounds* where smoking is permitted? That would

	lessen the fire risk and get rid of the smell and the smoke.
Jane Leggatt:	That little courtyard between the Science labs and the main building would be all right.
Mr Jarrold:	We'll be selling cigarettes in the tuckshop next.
Mrs Hurst:	I'm against the whole idea. I'm sure the staff won't like it.
Tom Reynolds:	Even the smokers. . .?
Mrs Hurst:	That's quite irrelevant. If they want to kill themselves, they're old enough to know the risks.
Headmaster:	I think I'll pass this one to the Parents' Association. By the way, Reynolds, had you an age limit in mind?
Tom Reynolds:	Yes, sir — twelve.
Mrs Hurst:	Why, that's virtually the whole school.
Headmaster:	I don't think that parents would approve of that. I was thinking in terms of fourteen myself.
Mr Jarrold:	That would let you in, wouldn't it, Reynolds?
Tom Reynolds:	I don't smoke, sir.
Headmaster:	Well, I'll have to think about this one. What's the next item on the agenda?
Mr Jarrold:	Pot in the playground.
Jane Leggatt:	Be serious, sir. The girls in my class think it would be a good idea if. . .

Main Points

When writing a précis, the hard work is done when you have selected and written down in your own words the chief ideas or main points as we usually call them. All that remains is to put these main points together in proper sentences within the limit of words stipulated. It is at this stage that the really skilful writer of précis will shine because he will have the ability to transform these bare bones into a piece of developed prose. As with most activities, facility comes with experience and this section gives you the opportunity of practising the final stage of précis-writing — fleshing out the skeleton and breathing life into it.

What the skilled writer will avoid are jerky, disconnected

summaries which lurch from one point to another without any coherent shape or progression. You cannot hope to out-write the original author who had the ideas and first choice of words in which to express them. But you can try to do justice to his argument or account by condensing it in clear, straightforward prose without falsification and without frills.

When it comes to précis work in exams, there will probably be an allocation of marks for selecting the main points and then a separate quota to be awarded for the style and general fluency of writing. It is this last aspect on which this section concentrates and the requirement in the pieces that follow is to take the main points listed and turn them into clear, connected English. Remember that there is no need to re-phrase the points which have been selected: imagine that this has already been done in the extraction process.

You will find helpful an awareness of certain connecting words. These will make easier the linking and, where necessary, contrasting of statements made in the main points. The obvious word to join two statements which point the same way is *and*; others which might be used are *furthermore* and *moreover*, and when you return to an argument after considering an argument on the other side *nevertheless* might be a useful term.

As far as changing the direction of an argument or narrative is concerned, the basic conjunction to use is *but*; alternatives include *however* (which in this sense will be marked off from the rest of the sentence by a comma or pair of commas) and *conversely*. One conjunction to be avoided is *therefore*. It is very popular among inexperienced précis-writers but should be confined to introducing the logical conclusion of a previous argument or statement that has been made. A much simpler word which is in general to be preferred is *so*, e.g.

so

I was out late last night (therefore) I had an extra hour in bed this morning.

In linking the main points you will, of course, try to be as economical as possible in your use of joining words. Phrases such as *in the first place* and *on the other hand*, while useful in certain types of writing, are too long-winded for summary. Try to use basic not bloated English.

There is no set limit of words in the exercises that follow. Nor is there a "correct" answer to each. The flexibility of the English language is such that several alternative versions may be entirely satisfactory. For instance, turn to Exercise 1 (p. 37) and read through the first five main points.

Numerous ways of combining these five pieces of information can be found and to give you some idea of the possibilities, here are four possible versions to consider.

i)   The aircraft had climbed to 3000 feet after take-off when a warning light on the control panel showed that there was a fire in the outer port engine so it was shut off and the extinguisher switched on, after which the plane turned round.

This version manages to combine all five statements into one sentence by the use of connecting words such as *when, that, so, and* and *after*. Words like these are very useful links. Can you spot any more in this second version?

ii)   The aircraft had climbed to 3000 feet after take-off but because a warning light on the control panel showed that there was a fire in the outer port engine, it was shut off, then the extinguisher was switched on and the plane turned round.

Of course, there is no need to incorporate the five main points into only one sentence. The next version packages the same information into two sentences.

iii)   Having climbed to 3000 feet after take-off, the aircraft turned round. A warning light on the control panel had shown that there was a fire in the outer port engine which was shut off and the extinguisher switched on.

The construction used at the beginning here (*Having climbed. . .*) is particularly valuable in summaries where you are trying to keep within a tight total. Notice also, towards the end, the link word *which*. Along with *who, whom* and *whose* this is a common connector of great value and versatility (*of which, on which, after which*, etc).

The final example illustrates how the main points can be expressed in three sentences.

iv)   When the aircraft had climbed to 3000 feet after take-off, a warning light showed on the control panel. The outer port engine was on fire so it was shut off and the extinguisher switched on. The plane then turned round.

Obviously, these four versions do not exhaust the possible permutations and you should be able to compose satisfactory alternatives without too much trouble. In fact, aim at starting Exercise 1 with your own individual version of the first five main points then carry on with the other six. In all the exercises

in this section try to turn the lists into good continuous prose as
briefly as you can.

1 Aircraft climbed to 3000 feet after take-off.
  Warning light showed on control panel.
  Fire in outer port engine.
  Engine shut off, extinguisher switched on.
  Plane turned round.
  Emergency landing, fire engines alongside.
  Passengers escaped down emergency shutes.
  All out in 90 seconds.
  Few bruises and sprains, otherwise fine.
  Passengers praised prompt action of crew.
  Delay of 4 hours before take-off in replacement plane.

2 Bugle sounded the charge.
  Gates of fort swung open.
  Cavalry, already formed up with drawn swords, galloped
  straight at circling Indians.
  Steady covering fire from entrance towers and stockade.
  Heavy casualties among cavalry as Indians reacted strongly.
  Cavalry pressed on towards Indian camp.
  More bugles heard in distance.
  Main force of troopers and artillery.
  Indians broke off attack, made towards hills.
  Great cheer from fort.

3 Learner-driver must first obtain necessary form from post
  office.
  Send it with fee to address stated.
  When provisional driving licence received, instruction with
  qualified driver or instructor.
  Study of Highway Code.
  When ready, fix driving test at one of Ministry centres.
  Practical test of driving competence, theoretical questions
  on Highway Code.
  Pass or fail; reasons for failure will be given.
  Free to drive unaccompanied if passed; take out full
  licence.

4 Writer argues that British spend far too much time
  watching sport.
  Greater variety of games played in U.K. than anywhere
  else on earth.
  Televised sport a bad influence.
  If all professional games players put to productive work,

trade gap could be narrowed.
Ridiculous that 11 grown men should be paid for trying to knock over 3 wooden sticks, while thousands watch.
Amounts gambled on horse-racing and football a scandal.
Invested in National Savings could transform economy.
True we need some relaxation but playing a hundred times better than watching.

5 Post Office advises that soft and unbreakable articles for posting should be wrapped in brown paper.
Anything else should be packed in rigid box.
Pack plenty of cushioning material round article to prevent interior movement.
Fasten parcel first with adhesive tape then string placed round in at least 2 directions.
Make sure parcel is clearly and accurately addressed.
Don't use tie-on label only; stick-on one also necessary.
Fragile articles should be labelled accordingly.
Perishable goods may not be sent by letter post.
Must be packed to prevent leakage and suitably labelled.
No guarantee of delivery within specified period.

6 Pennsylvania in N E of U S A.
Area 45000 square miles, population 11½ million.
Capital Harrisburg.
Principal rivers the Delaware, Susquehanna and Ohio.
Climate humid continental type; annual rainfall 35-50 ins.
Extensive forests; main agricultural products hay, vegetables, fruit.
Rich in minerals, especially coal.
Iron and steel industry centred on Pittsburgh produces 30% of total U.S. output.
Philadelphia, 4th largest city in USA, is great textile centre.
State originally settled by Swedes then by Dutch.
William Penn granted extensive lands in 1681, named them Pennsylvania (Penn's woods).

The Right Order

In general when writing a précis it is best to retain the order in which the original information is presented. The writer had a clear idea of what he wanted to convey and presumably arranged his material in the most effective way, sentence by sentence, paragraph by paragraph. In normal exposition (writing that sets out to explain) you will find that the first sentence of a paragraph usually makes an important statement which is then developed and illustrated during the rest of the paragraph. In informative writing of this kind, then, it pays the précis writer to give particular attention to the initial sentences of paragraphs as these often give a skeleton outline of the main drift or argument of the passage. Re-arranging these topic sentences, as they are sometimes called, would only confuse the issue.

This principle of retaining the original structure, however, does not always hold good for writing which is less concerned with conveying information than with creating impressions and moods and feelings. This is the purpose behind much imaginative and descriptive writing, the kind which is often found in novels. Here an author may embed his solid building-block statements in a mass of supporting suggestion and evocative detail. It is the job of the précis-writer to reduce this luxuriant growth to order and shape; he will lose much of the flavour and atmosphere but these are qualities which do not concern the summarist.

The three extracts that follow are deliberately descriptive and there is no clear sequence from A to B to C. Look out for the key sentence in each piece, the one that specifies what the passage is about. It will not be the one that is printed first but when you have spotted it, use it as the starting point for your summary. It will fix the time, the place, the occasion — the sort of details that a reader in a hurry needs to set him off on the road to quick understanding. After this definite start you can continue with whatever information you consider to be important but you will aim at plain statements without the elaboration of the original.

i) Summarise the passage that follows in about 60 words.

Hundreds of youths in blue and white scarves were thrusting into the ground through turnstiles down below and mounting the steep steps that led to the terraces. There was an air of expectancy all round the ground, a buzz of voices, the feeling of anticipation that is often sharper than disappointed reality. At the far end, across the spruce turf, greener than any farmer's field, the predominant colours were red and white. They seized the eye, as scarves, held aloft between out-stretched arms, were moved from side to side in unison. Rival chants already split the air, drowning even the distorted music which blared out over the loudspeakers. Most of the seats in the stands were already occupied, breathing space on the terraces was fast disappearing. There were ten minutes to go before kick-off in the opening match of the season: United v. City — what a way to start the year!

ii)   Write a summary of this extract from a science fiction novel in no more than 50 words.

In the stone galleries the people were gathered in clusters and groups filtering up into shadows among the blue hills. A soft evening light shone over them from the stars and the luminous double moons of Mars. Beyond the marble amphitheatre, in darkness and distances, lay little towns and villas; pools of silver water stood motionless and canals glittered from horizon to horizon. It was an evening in summer upon the placid and temperate planet Mars. Up and down green wine canals, boats as delicate as bronze flowers drifted. In the long and endless dwellings that curved like tranquil snakes across the hills, lovers lay idly whispering in cool night beds. The last children ran in torchlit alleys, gold spiders in their hands throwing out films of web. Here or there a late supper was prepared in tables where lava bubbled silvery and hushed. In the amphitheatres of a hundred towns on the night side of Mars the brown Martian people with gold coin eyes were leisurely met to fix their attention on stages where musicians made a serene music flow up like blossom scent on the still air.

iii)   Summarise the following passage in no more than 70 words.

Outside the sun shines down from an unclouded sky. Every window is opened fully to catch the slightest breeze that might blow. Summer sounds drift in from each side while at the back of the hall an electric clock whirrs away, slightly out of sorts. There they sit, on the hottest day of the year, the exam candidates, row upon row of scribblers, this year's victims in the annual initiation rites. Here and there a girl gazes into the distance to be startled out of her daydream by a prolific hand shooting up for yet another sheet of continuation paper. Anxious eyes consult the clock: thirty minutes to go and two questions yet to be attempted. A few have given up, beaten by the heat or their own inadequacy. "Will I get a mark if I write my name and number neatly?" One restless invigilator, in striped cotton frock, pads up and down the rows like a caged tiger; the other two seem to have nodded off at their desks, oblivious to the snapping fingers seeking ink or paper or, perhaps, permission to leave this teenage torture-chamber. In half an hour it will all be over, scripts collected, tension released in hubbub, pennies belatedly dropping. Then the clean sweep of brooms, the smell of antiseptic sawdust, the banging of windows and the turning of the lock on Day One of the infernal, eternal, external exams.

Six Short Summaries

You should now be ready to put together all the stages of summary-writing that we have practised so far. In this section you are asked to write six short précis following the complete drill established in previous pages. So it's i) read the passage until its meaning is clear; ii) note the main points in your own words; iii) write them up in continuous prose; iv) check that you are inside the word limit; v) if necessary, shorten your summary by crossing out inessentials or re-phrasing; vi) write out a final "fair copy" and put the total of words used in brackets at the end.

When arriving at your total, remember that the length of a word is immaterial: both "I" and "floccinaucinihilipilification" count as one word. Note, however, that compound words (two words joined by a hyphen) are counted as single words, e.g. full-back, harbour-master, ice-cream.

The instructions for each of the pieces that follow are the same. Write a précis of the passage within the limit of words indicated. Show your list of main points and put the total of words used at the end of your final version.

i)   Travel is the best education. You soon become proficient at Maths when you have to change your pounds into drachmas, escudos, francs, guilders or whatever. And checking restaurant bills and hotel accounts with 5% added on for this and 10% for that is the best incentive for accurate arithmetic. If you get the answer wrong it's your pocket that suffers. It is obvious, too, that the only way to learn a foreign language is to go and mingle with the natives. Working your way page by page through a grammar book even if it's supplemented by a weekly session in the language lab is a poor substitute. The same goes for Geography: words, photos, slides, films — they're only second-best. Seeing for yourself is believing. And there's nothing like ambling round the Acropolis or climbing up the Colosseum to bring home History. Nor need you neglect your Science. Every country you visit is a living lesson in Botany and Zoology and as you watch the wings of your aircraft flex and hear the note of its engine change while it comes in to land on some foreign runway, you'll be able to muse on the wonders of modern technology.

(Limit: 70 words)

ii)   An officer came presently, when night had fallen, and inspected the crowd on the veranda in the light of a hurricane lamp; he walked down the veranda thrusting his lamp forward at each group, a couple of soldiers hard on his heels with rifles at the ready and bayonets fixed. Most of the children started crying. The inspection finished, he made a little speech in broken English. "Now you are prisoners," he said. "You stay here tonight. Tomorrow you go to prisoner camp perhaps. You do good things, obedience to orders, you will receive good from Japanese soldiers. You do bad things, you will be shot directly. So, do good things always. When officer come, you stand up and bow, always. That is good thing. Now you sleep."

One of the men asked, "May we have beds and mosquito nets?"

"Japanese soldiers have no beds, no mosquito nets. Perhaps tomorrow you have beds and nets."

Another said, "Can we have some supper?" This had to be explained. "Food."

"Tomorrow you have food." The officer walked away, leaving two sentries on guard at each end of the veranda.

(Limit: 65 words)

iii)   New Delhi, India's capital, is a modern city with wide avenues, palatial Government offices, ultra-modern blocks of flats, and air-conditioned houses. Yet the very moment one leaves the capital one is transported into the Middle Ages, into a world of bullock carts, mud houses, and Persian wheels turned by camels and bullocks, who go round and round pulling the water out of the soil along a wooden wheel studded with rusty buckets; at night the huts are lit by the flicker of kerosene lamps, in sharp contrast to the floodlit capital. Bombay provides a greater contrast still, with its prosperous mills, its busy port, its modern offices, its atomic energy research station — one of the most advanced in the world — and its electric trains. Bombay is a modern industrial town, yet a few miles away from the atomic research station there are aboriginal tribes who live in mud villages, armed with bows and arrows, eating what they can fish or shoot to supplement the produce of the simplest kind of farming. India's modern towns are a subject of wonder to the villagers when they come, barefoot or in sandalled feet, riding on the front edge of their bullock carts, while women and children pile in the back of the cart atop of the produce of the land which is being taken to the market.

(Limit: 80 words)

iv)   Blustering March winds buffeted the walls of a mansion close to the Charterhouse Priory in the City of London. On one of the window seats, her tapestry in her hands — although she was paying little attention to the design she was working — sat a woman. She was small and her hair, which was fair and abundant, showed beneath her hood of black velvet; her gown of the same material was richly embroidered, but in dark colours; and the skirt was open in the front to display her silk petticoat, which was a sombre shade of purple; the long veil flowing from the back of her headdress proclaimed her a widow. Her face was charming, but the charm came from its expression rather than a regularity of features; at the moment it seemed to wear a borrowed beauty; her cheeks were flushed, her eyes bright, and it was as though this beauty had snatched away ten years of her thirty and made her a young woman of twenty again.

She was in love; and the eager glances which she cast down at the courtyard suggested that she was waiting for her lover.

(Limit: 70 words)

v)

10, West Street,
Edinburgh.
1st July 1977

Miss Jayne MacBayne,
6, The Drive,
Newton.

Dear Miss MacBayne,
We regret to inform you that your aunt, Mrs Martha Dunn, passed away on the 15th June, 1977 after a short illness. As executors of her will, it is our duty to apprise you that you are entitled to the residue of her estate after some small legacies to her housekeeper and staff, together with some minor disbursements, have been paid.

It will be necessary for you to attend our office in person to produce proof of identity such as your birth certificate or passport. May we suggest that you telephone this office for an appointment at your early convenience when we will be pleased to supply fuller details of the properties, goods, chattels and cash in hand which you may expect to receive, subject, of course, to the deduction of the appropriate duty and legal expenses.

> I am,
> Yours truly,
> for Hunter, Scott and Hunter,
> J.S. Hinchcliffe

(Limit: 60 words)

vi)   With our wide range of materials and fuels it is difficult to remember the enormous importance of wood in pre-industrial Britain. It was the chief material for the construction of most things man made, and for centuries was his only fuel. This need of wood combined with the spread of farming produced a steady destruction of the original forest cover of Britain, and despite the Norman Forest Laws and the enclosure of private hunting-parks the long-term process was everywhere the same — the conversion of woodland to open country, whether arable or grazing. This increasing shortage of trees was recognized as serious even in the Middle Ages, and down the centuries responsible people tried vainly to prevent the wholesale loss of timber reserves. Sheep, however, were England's wealth in the Middle Ages, and sheep are most efficient converters of forest to grassland. Britain became grassier. The Black Death reduced the number of labourers for arable farming and pasture replaced corn. Britain became grassier still. The population recovered and farming spread into areas formerly wild like the North-West, destroying the forests as it spread. Britain became a naval power and more trees were felled for ship-building. Glass-making and iron-smelting became widespread and burned up the woodlands for fuel, until even the ancient impenetrable forest of Andreada on the Wealden clay was gradually eroded by the iron-founders.

(Limit: 80 words)

Selective Summary

So far, we have concentrated on preliminary practice for formal précis work where a whole passage has to be shortened. In this section the emphasis is on *selective* summary, i.e. only certain aspects of the original will be involved. Your first task, however, will still be to read all the passage carefully for you must understand the whole before you concentrate on the parts relevant to your answer. When you know what the passage is about, turn to the instructions and read them with extra care because you must have clearly in your mind just what it is you are looking for before you begin looking.

In the shorter paragraphs that follow, you will probably be able to give the required summary without any preliminary notes. But as the passages grow more complex you will have to jot down the main points that you will want to incorporate in your final version. Remember, again, to re-phrase the relevant material: copying out chunks of the original will not do.

i) There is much to be said for a cat as a pet. Unlike many dogs it will not have a voracious appetite nor will there be any problem of exercising it. Cats are clean animals and are easily house-trained. They have distinctive characters and an engaging independence which make them altogether superior to fish or birds as companions. The necessity in the average home to confine birds to cages is a drawback: birds cost little to feed, are colourful, cheerful and good company especially for an old house-bound person. But a cat will become one of the family in a way that no fish or bird can ever be.

Summarise as briefly as you can what this passage has to say about birds as pets.

ii) The trend towards comprehensive schools is now irreversible. The number of grammar schools still functioning diminishes each year and the same is true of secondary moderns. The rigorous academic training of an intellectual elite formerly undertaken by the grammar schools is being increasingly replaced in the all-ability schools by courses of a wider and less demanding nature. The study of the classics, which was a strong tradition in the grammar schools, is now declining sharply.

Summarise briefly what you have learned from this passage about grammar schools.

iii)   One Friday evening Sullivan and his four boxers were displaying themselves in the blazing light of the big electric lamps hanging over the platform outside the show. The fair was flashing and whirling and quivering with light. Between the shows moved a dark flock of people. There was an air of gaiety and great excitement in the shrieking and laughing and shouting of voices, the brassy music of the big roundabout, the crack of rifle shots and the thunder of switchback cars, which never seemed to rest. The night was sultry, without wind, and above the electric lights the summer darkness, freckled with tiny stars, was coming down a soft dark blue.

In one sentence summarise what this extract tells us about the noise of the fair.

iv)   Before the end of the century mankind will have to find new sources of energy or else develop new techniques to exploit existing ones which have not yet been fully utilised. Oil has increased in price so rapidly and so much that it is no longer a cheap fuel. Nor is coal and known reserves of both are fast being used up. Scientists will increasingly turn to the sun, the winds and the tides as sources of energy and efforts to unlock and harness the atom will doubtless be intensified.

Explain in no more than 15 words why, according to this passage, new sources of energy will have to be developed soon.

v)   One of the first necessities of life for any animal is food, and by reason of their colossal size elephants make very large demands in this respect. In fact the quantity of food consumed by a single elephant in one day is so enormous that it is a cause of perennial astonishment even to those who have long been familiar with the animal. In British and American zoos and circuses a full-grown elephant will eat about 100 lbs. of hay a day, supplemented by bran, oats, and root vegetables, and as many buns as benevolent visitors can be persuaded to part with. The diet can be reduced for some months of the year to about 75 lbs. of hay, or even less, but as soon as the intake falls below this level there is a danger that the animal will lose condition. Moreover, the reduced diet applies only to resting animals, and is quite inadequate if the elephant is to be heavily worked. Another factor to bear in mind is that zoo and circus elephants are usually females; for full-grown bulls the figures must be at least doubled. Elephants in the wild eat much larger quantities of food, as a limitless supply is readily available. They seem to prefer green shoots, leaves, and tender twigs to grass, and it is therefore doubtful whether the hay that forms the staple diet of elephants in captivity arouses them to any special gastronomic enthusiasm.

In no more than 35 words, summarise what you have learned from this extract about the diet of elephants in captivity.

vi)   Of all the sports and activities available in this country, swimming is perhaps the most convenient and beneficial. The whole body is exercised in a most refreshing way, yet without stress and without strain. Unlike many outdoor and indoor games there are no teams required with so many a side having to be mustered before one can really enjoy oneself. It is possible to swim on one's own and still derive much pleasure from the activity — although being with friends will add to the enjoyment. Nor is it expensive — unlike such games as golf and squash which often involve hefty subscriptions. If you live at the sea-side, of course, or near an unpolluted lake or river it need cost you nothing. Another advantage of swimming is that no costly equipment is needed, no sets of expensive clubs, no elaborate kit. You can even swim without a costume if you pick your time and place! The one snag with swimming is that it can be dangerous if you over-reach yourself or take risks but even when you cross the road there is no guarantee that you will reach the other side.

Summarise in about 40 words the advantages of swimming as outlined in this extract.

vii)   The weather was getting noticeably colder and the wind more boisterous though still variable. We were getting close to the Roaring Forties and I started to prepare *Suhaili* as well as I could for what I expected to come. I removed any unnecessary gear from the deck such as running poles and spare sheets and stowed these below. I sealed off every opening such as the engine control box and the forward hatch-way, and also put more seam stopper round the sky-light, which was still leaking. August in the Southern Hemisphere is equivalent to February in the north. I could expect some pretty rough weather and I wanted *Suhaili* as ready as possible to take it. I went through all the stores, giving priority now to storm sails, spare lashing for emergencies, the sea anchor and warp and anything that I might need in a hurry. I put all my tropical clothing at the bottom of the sail bag I used as a wardrobe, and put sweaters, jeans, shirts and socks at the top. Finally I topped up my ready-use polythene containers in the main cabin with petrol and paraffin from forward.

In no more than 35 words, summarise the preparations described by the narrator in this excerpt.

viii)   Corfu lies off the Albanian and Greek coast-lines like a long, rust-eroded scimitar. The hilt of the scimitar is the mountain region of the island, for the most part barren and stony with towering rock cliffs haunted by blue-rock thrushes and peregrine falcons. In the valleys in this mountain region, however, where water gushed plentifully from the red and gold rocks, you would get forests of almond and walnut trees, casting shade as cool as a well, thick battalions of spear-like cypress and silver-trunked fig trees with leaves as large as a salver. The blade of the scimitar is made up of rolling greeny-silver eiderdowns of giant olives, some reputedly over five hundred years old and each one unique in its hunched, arthritic shape, its trunk pitted with a hundred holes like pumice stone. Towards the tip of the blade you had Lefkimi with its twinkling, eye-aching sand dunes and great salt marshes, decorated with acres of bamboos that creaked and rustled and whispered to each other surreptitiously.

Write a summary of all that you have learned from this passage about the vegetation of Corfu. Use no more than 40 words.

ix)   The advantages of travelling to the other countries of Europe by air are obvious. The further one has to go, the greater is the time saved; one is guaranteed a seat in relative comfort; the standards of service are good; and punctuality is much improved. Critics maintain that air travel is expensive and the baggage allowance restricting but this must be set against the fact that one is spared the ordeal of boarding a boat and entrusting oneself to the tender mercies of the English Channel or, worse still, the North Sea. It is true that some people are scared stiff of flying and that flights are sometimes delayed by bad weather but the business men and tourists who throng the airports throughout the year are not deterred by the knowledge that sooner or later another air disaster will hit the headlines.

In about 25 words, outline what this paragraph has to say on the snags of air travel in Europe.

x)   As nearly perfect at self-subsistence as any fighting man in the world's history was the Apache warrior, even though his chosen campaigning ground was ferociously sterile desert. No clumsy supply column accompanied him, nor any pots, frying pans or other utensils, save for the knife sheathed at his belt. In addition to the white man's sheep and cattle, which he took without hesitation or qualm of conscience, his range was the habitat of many kinds of game — deer, *javalinas* (desert peccaries), rabbits, wild turkey and desert mountain sheep. Nor was he dainty in his tastes. When other meat lacked he did not disdain mice or pack rats, dug from their small lairs, or lizards killed with a switch, or even the grey flesh of the coiling rattlesnake. When all else failed, his pony was always a last resource. Killed when perhaps too exhausted to move farther, it furnished a stock of jerked meat* and a unique water carrier — the long intestine, which, cleaned (after somewhat rudimentary Apache notions of cleaning), could be filled with water and wound several times about the body of another horse, to furnish life-giving if somewhat offensively smelling and tasting water for days. It is no wonder that the frontier troops, handicapped by pack trains and equipment, had difficulty in coping with their wily and resourceful foe.
* strips of meat dried in the sun

Explain in about 40 words how the Apache warrior was able to survive in the desert.

xi)   Kino was in mid-leap when the gun crashed and the barrel-flash made a picture on his eyes. The great knife swung and crunched hollowly. It bit through neck and deep into chest, and Kino was a terrible machine now. He grasped the rifle even as he wrenched free his knife. His strength and his movement and his speed were a machine. He whirled and struck the head of the seated man like a melon. The third man scrabbled away like a crab, slipped into the pool, and then he began to climb frantically, to climb up the cliff where the water pencilled down. His hands and feet threshed in the tangle of the wild grapevine, and he whimpered and gibbered as he tried to get up. But Kino had become as cold and deadly as steel. Deliberately he threw the lever of the rifle, and then he raised the gun and aimed deliberately and fired. He saw his enemy tumble backwards into the pool, and Kino strode to the water. In the moonlight he could see the frantic frightened eyes, and Kino aimed and fired between the eyes.

Summarise in no more than 30 words how the third man tried to escape and how Kino killed him.

xii)   Hitler always had an air of sincerity, and at these early meetings, in particular, there was also an air of innocence to him, almost of naivety. It brought out paternal and maternal feelings to see this young war veteran, with the Iron Cross, expressing himself so passionately and with such a love for his country. He was the voice from the trenches. He marched into the meeting room as if stamping on to parade; although he wore civilian clothes he was, with his stiff bearing, his cropped hair and his narrow, trimmed-back moustache, the epitome of an N.C.O. He began his speech standing stiffly to attention, his chin up. When his throaty, deep voice had caught the attention of his audience, he began to relax and to use gestures; he liked to spread out his hands and rock gently from side to side. He used rough humour, often in the form of an imaginary dialogue in which he stated an opponent's case and then answered it. With variations in pace and style, he could hold an audience for an hour or even two hours. He planted questioners in his audience to "feed" him. It was, really, a form of dramatic performance; both from instinct and experience he learned to get at an audience's emotions rather than to persuade it by a logical chain of argument. Finally he worked himself up into a peroration, his hoarse voice breaking in passion, his arms moving in sweeping gestures; he finished with a command like a whip-lash: "Germany awake!" The veins on his face stood out, his eyes bulged and he was drenched in sweat. Then he would take a swig of beer (he was not yet a complete teetotaller) and leave the hall as soon as he could. Apart from the fact that he was emotionally drained, he came to believe that it was tactically an anti-climax for a speaker to hang around chatting normally. He cultivated an air of mystery about himself and refused to be photographed.

Summarise what you have learned from this passage about Hitler's technique of speech-making. (Max. 65 words)

Final Versions

You will sometimes find when writing a summary that, having selected the main points, your first attempt at incorporating them into a connected version is well outside the limit of words allowed. You must then revise the final version, re-wording and pruning so that you keep the essential information but with more economical wording. This section gives you practice in this final slimming process which is often necessary when summarising passages of several hundred words.

To give you some idea of what can be achieved, compare these two summaries. No. 1 is a first attempt at reducing an extract of 380 words to 120. As it stands, it contains 156 words and so must be trimmed by 36. No. 2 is a shorter version of exactly 120 words. Compare the two, sentence by sentence, and see how the saving in words has been made. As a basis for comparison, the number of words per sentence has been printed in both versions.

1   In some ways raising the school leaving age to sixteen has not been a success. (15) A great number of pupils who are not academically inclined have simply stayed away from school and either taken unofficial jobs or hung around street corners wasting their time. (29) The authorities in some areas have been slow to prosecute because of the fact that by the time proceedings could be brought, the boy or girl in question would have been old enough to leave school legally. (37) Nor have schools gone out of their way to have back in the class-room reluctant and often disruptive pupils whose one aim has been to get themselves suspended. (28) Another snag has been that young people whose sixteenth birthday falls before the end of January have been allowed to leave at Easter, a ruling which has meant that there was no incentive for them to stay on to take an external examination in May or June. (47)

2   Raising the school leaving age to sixteen has been a partial failure. (12) Many pupils, not academically inclined, have simply truanted, taking unofficial jobs or hanging around street corners wasting their time. (19) Some local authorities have been slow to prosecute because by the time proceedings could be brought, the offenders would have been old enough to leave school legally. (27) Nor have schools been over-anxious to have back in the classroom reluctant and often disruptive pupils whose one aim was to get themselves suspended. (24) Another snag has been that young people whose sixteenth birthday falls before January 31st have been allowed to leave at Easter which was no incentive for them to stay on to take an external examination in the summer. (38)

In comparing these two versions, remember that this is only one way of achieving the necessary reduction and that many alternative ways could be just as satisfactory. Sometimes, for instance, two sentences can be combined at a considerable saving. In this example, however, note particularly how i) a positive statement is shorter than a negative one: *not a success = a failure* (1st sentence); ii) many phrases can be replaced by single words: *a great number of* = *many* (2nd sentence); iii) relative pronouns — who, which and that — and their verbs often give scope for shortcuts (2nd sentence); iv) some phrases can simply be omitted with no loss of meaning: *of the fact that* (3rd sentence).

Now try your hand at the three pieces that follow. In each case you are shown the total of words used and given the target that has to be reached. Remember that it should not be necessary to make drastic changes or dramatic cuts: an average of 4 or 5 words per sentence will usually do the trick.

i) The Count, who had been a prisoner for a period of six years, used to pace up and down his cell during the hours of darkness. This action had the effect of intensely annoying his gaoler, who complained that it prevented him from getting any sleep. After the gaoler had complained many times, the Count came up with a suggestion. He remarked that it might not be a bad idea if he were to be given a bottle of wine with his evening meal. Wine, which often made other men noisy and obstreperous, always resulted in making him sleepy. The gaoler grumbled that it was against all the rules but that he would go to any lengths to get a good night's sleep. From then on, the nocturnal pacing no longer occurred and prisoner and guard slept without disturbance.

(Total: 139 words. Reduce to 110.)

ii) Young people in their teens are a mass of contradictions. They say that they do not want to be forced to wear uniform at school and yet as soon as they get home in the evening they change out of one uniform into another — jeans and tee-shirt — which they have chosen themselves. They are anxious to show how independent they are and this they demonstrate by congregating together in large numbers, listening to the same music and dressing identically in the latest fashion decreed by the unnamed manipulators who milk the teenage market. There is in all probability a greater gap between this generation and their parents than has ever existed in the history of the world. In previous centuries a man passed on his skills to his sons and his wife educated their daughters.

Now the job has been given to the professional educators and the result is cultural chaos.

(Total: 151 words. Reduce to 120.)

iii)   Gardening must be one of the most satisfying hobbies that a man or woman can have. Whether one grows flowers or vegetables or just grass, a tremendous amount of pleasure can be derived from the finished product. The beauty of a flower garden, the orderly rows of carrots and cabbages, the smoothness of a rolled and mown lawn — these are the quiet satisfactions known to thousands in every county in England. Then there are the sensual and material rewards: the scent of freshly cut roses in the sitting-room, the flavour of one's own potatoes and peas, the peace of tea on the lawn under the shade of fruit trees that one has planted oneself. We are told that when God looked at his finished creation he liked it for it was good. Each of us lucky enough to own a small patch of earth can experience that same feeling when we contemplate a garden that we have planned, toiled in, nurtured and brought to fruition. The fact that we have calloused hands, chronic backache and blackfly in the beans is a minor irritation.

(Total: 183 words. Reduce to 140.)

Connected Paragraphs

The following account tells how Londoners reacted to the Great Plague of 1665. Although it is a connected description, it has been printed as a series of separate paragraphs. Summarise each paragraph in turn, using no more than the number of words shown. When you have completed each summary you have only to link them — with suitable connecting words where necessary — and you will have a précis of the whole.

When you are faced with longer passages, as you will be in the pages that follow, do not be intimidated by the bulk of the material. Treat it as a series of separate paragraphs and deal with them one at a time as you have practised in previous sections. Instead of three or four main points you will gradually build up to nine or ten but the principle is the same and you will soon become accustomed to the idea that mere length does not make for difficulty. Instead, you will have the satisfaction of producing summaries that can be polished pieces of writing with enough development in them to create interest.

Soon the roads out of London, in all directions, like the spokes of a great wheel with the City at the centre, were thick with traffic. It moved slowly with much creaking of axles and leather harnesses; then, as now on the narrow English roads, there was little room for the faster carriages to pass the slow unsprung carts. Beggars with crutches, poor families with their belongings bundled on their backs in blankets, servants for whom there was no room in the carriages; all these clogged the roads on either side of the coaches. Sometimes someone, already ill with plague or struck with weariness or age, fell in the dust. No-one stopped to succour such unfortunates. They were pushed to one side into the thick, dry, speary grass to die or to recover. If anyone thought they had anything valuable on them — a ring, a purse, a coin — they were stripped and robbed and left naked to the sky.

(Limit: 50 words)

There were not many heroes in London during that spring, summer and autumn: the urge for self-preservation, for survival in a city of the dying and the dead, stripped away the thin shells of conscience and kindness. Everyone was for themselves; to stay alive was all that mattered; how they did so was their own affair. Clergy abandoned their parishes without a thought, doctors their patients, landlords their tenants, and the rich their dependants.

(Limit: 25 words)

Many wealthy families decided to leave their London homes locked and bolted, with all windows shuttered, during their absence. In these circumstances they could see no point in continuing to pay servants who had nothing to do. They therefore dismissed them at the moment their own carriages started to move. Those who were discarded in this way followed the coach for a little way either begging their masters to reconsider their decision, or cursing them, according to age, sex and temperament. They had no chance of finding any other employment at such a time. They were literally left in the street outside the locked houses, without refuge, without food, without hope, facing the alternatives of starving to death or dying of plague.

(Limit: 35 words)

It was from these wretched and abandoned creatures that parishes found some to drive the two- and four-wheeled carts — the 'dead-carts' — to collect the corpses of plague victims.

Others roamed the streets looking for empty houses to loot or lonely pedestrians to rob. Since many London households contained between thirty and fifty servants, these desperate characters became a serious and constant problem during that year and for some time afterwards.

(Limit: 35 words)

4

Over To You

If you have worked conscientiously through the previous sections of this book, you should now be prepared to write summaries of any length — and, in particular, of the types which are set in examinations in English language. The remainder of the material in the pages that follow consists of a variety of passages for summarising. Some require a précis of the whole, others demand a more flexible and selective approach, involving only certain aspects of the original. If your main aim in using the book is to prepare for the exam of a particular Board, then you may wish to concentrate on the passages which give practice in the type of question you will meet. If you are aiming to sharpen your summarising skills in a more general way then you should attempt a cross-section of the remaining exercises which are graded in difficulty, the last ones being of external exam standard.

1   Write a summary of the passage which follows in no more than 80 words. You will find that it contains quite a lot of details, sometimes in the form of lists. When you have read the passage once to find its general meaning, go back through it and look for the lists. Remember that in your summary you will replace them by general expressions or, if they are examples of something already mentioned, you can omit them altogether.

The North American wheat harvest begins in Texas, in mid-May. By the time it is finished, in October, thousands of combine-harvesters will have chewed their way north for 2,000 miles — to the Canadian prairies.

As the Texas green ripens to yellow, combine crews (they call themselves contract or "custom" cutters) converge from every wheat state in the west: from Montana and the Dakotas, from Wyoming and Nebraska, from Kansas and Colorado.

Rumbling down from Oklahoma comes a convoy of 20 vehicles: trucks, combines, pick-ups, caravans. The boss, the owner of the whole circus, is Dale Starks. He first made this journey 27 years ago — with a bank loan and one secondhand combine. He has been coming back every year ever since. Today, he owns nine combines. They will be contract-cutting for the next seven months — five on wheat, two on maize.

A few of Starks's men are old hands at the work, but many of them are only 18 or 19 years old and have never driven a combine before. Some are doing it for the money, some because they want to try something new. They come from all over: cities, farms, factories and colleges.

The combines, which cost 23,000 dollars apiece, each weigh ten tons, have automatic gears, power steering, two-way radio and air-conditioned cabs. Each of them can harvest enough wheat in an hour to keep the average four-person family in bread for 40 years.

2   Summarise this passage in no more than 75 words. Remember to give the substance of the conversation in reported speech.

At about half past eight o'clock on Tuesday morning a small boy paused on the pavement edge of a busy crossing in Birmingham, and watched the policeman directing the traffic. When that ahead of him was held up he crossed to the middle of the road, stationed himself alongside the policeman, waiting patiently to be attended to. Presently, his traffic safely on course for the moment, the policeman bent down.

"Hullo, Sonny, and what's your trouble?" he enquired.

"Please, sir," said the boy, "I'm afraid I'm sort of lost. And it's difficult because I haven't any money to get home with."

The policeman shook his head.

"That's bad," he said, sympathetically. "And where would home be?"

"Hindmere," the boy told him.

The policeman stiffened, and looked at him with sudden interest.

"And what's your name?" he asked, carefully.

"Matthew," said Matthew. "Matthew Gore."

"Is it, begod!" said the policeman. "Now you stand just where you are, Matthew. Don't move an inch."

He took a microphone out of his breast-pocket, pressed a switch, and spoke into it.

A squad car drew up beside them a couple of minutes later.

"That's service for you. Come to take you home. Hop in now," the policeman told him.

"Thank you very much, sir," said Matthew, with his customary respect for the police.

3   The following table shows the results of a survey carried out in Fairside Comprehensive School to find the pupils' views on the effectiveness of various disciplinary measures. Study the table carefully then write a report summarising the findings, using no more than 100 words.

Disciplinary measure	Number who considered it most effective		
	Girls	Boys	Total
Corporal punishment	142	110	252
Extra work	60	90	150
Detention after school	95	80	175
Writing lines	2	6	8
Loss of privileges	10	20	30
Picking up litter	20	7	27
Letter to parents	80	120	200
Interview with Head	116	95	211
	525	528	1053

4   Write a summary of the following extract in no more than 80 words.

Shortly before midnight on Saturday, September 1st, 1666, Thomas Farynor, King Charles's baker, and his daughter Hannah, climbed the rickety stairs from the bakery to their bedroom in their wood-framed house in Pudding Lane, near London Bridge.

Two hours later they were awake, gasping and choking in thick clouds of acrid smoke that billowed up these stairs. A pile of faggots and dry brushwood for the oven had somehow caught alight; the whole ground floor was an inferno.

Farynor quickly realised that escape down the stairs was impossible, so, seizing his daughter's arm, he pulled her to a garret window and helped her out on to the roof. Then, calling to his two servants to follow him, he climbed out himself. His manservant obeyed; the other, a maid, stayed behind screaming in terror, as afraid of the height as of the fire.

Hunched up, on hands and feet, the three frightened people crept over the tiles to the roof of the house next door. They reached this and then realised that the maid was not with them. By then it was too late for them to go back for her. Their house and bakery was aroar with flames; the maid's screams of terror were soon drowned by the crash of falling beams.

Thus, in that hour, as the capital slept, the Great Fire of London began, and claimed its first life.

5   In no more than 80 words, summarise what the following passage tells us about the differences between Willie Bond and Willie Marchant.

If you live at Thrush Green you can expect your morning post between 7.30 and 8.15 a.m.

If it is Willie Bond's week to deliver the letters, then they will be early. But if Willie Marchant is the postman then it is no use fretting and fuming. The post will arrive well after eight o'clock, and you may as well resign yourself to the fact.

"It just shows you can't go by looks," Thrush Green residents tell each other frequently. Willie Bond weighs fifteen stone, is short-legged and short-necked, and puffs in a truly alarming fashion as he pushes his bicycle up the steep hill from the post office at Lulling. His eyes are mere slits in the pink and white moon of his chubby face, and his nickname of Porky is still used by those who were his schoolfellows.

Willie Marchant, on the other hand, is a gaunt bean-pole of a fellow with a morose, lined face and a cigarette stub in the corner of his mouth. He scorns to dismount at Thrush Green's sharp hill, but tacks purposefully back and forth across the road with a fine disregard for the motorists who suffer severe shock when coming upon him suddenly at his manoeuvres. He was once knocked off his bicycle as he made a sharp right-hand turn from one bank to the other, but escaped with a bruised knee and a torn trouser leg.

6   Write a summary of the following passage in about 100 words.

The motor-car has made most cities unbearable to live in. Apart from the continuous noise of its infernal combustion engine, it is responsible for the worst fraction of the atmospheric pollution. It fills the streets with poisonous carbon monoxide and tetraethyl lead, which might be responsible for the sluggishness and frayed tempers of the citizens of London, Los Angeles, New York and Tokyo. Many main city thoroughfares have almost lethal concentrations of toxic gases during the hours of greatest human activity. At traffic lights when engines are idling the production of carbon monoxide goes up and the alertness of the drivers goes down. In the next decade, if the number of vehicles continues to increase, the carbon monoxide levels might be such that many streets will be too dangerous for pedestrians to use during the day, particularly in summer months — the streets will become canyons of death. But instead of banning the motor-car from the cities the trend has been to make the city more accommodating to it. Millions of pounds and hundreds of hours have been swallowed up in devising flow systems for traffic, but comparatively little money and time have been devoted to eliminating the gases, noise and the physical and mental strain imposed by the motor-car. The priority accorded to the motor vehicle was demonstrated in 1970 with the opening of the £30 million Westway extension of London's Western Avenue. At this point the elevated road, which took four years to build, is on average thirty feet from the rows of terraced houses where the residents were already subjected to the scream of jet airliners passing overhead and the rumble of underground trains below. The road was built to carry thousands of vehicles a day through some of the most over-crowded housing in London. No wonder the residents carried banners with the slogan "Get us out of this hell!" The planners ignored people!

7 In no more than 60 words, explain what you have learned about duelling pistols from this extract.

Duelling as a means of settling a quarrel, especially one of honour, had a long history. It was even used as a means of deciding guilt. When fencing was developed, rapiers became a popular duelling weapon but their use required a degree of skill not possessed by all and soon the pistol was rivalling the sword as a duelling weapon.

At first it was just a matter of using any convenient pair of pistols but towards the end of the eighteenth century there began to develop a pistol designed exclusively for duelling. What was wanted was a pistol with a fairly short range but which was as accurate and reliable as possible and which came up to the aim with little bother.

In Britain it was not considered sporting or desirable to

have rifled duelling pistols but the Continent seems not to have been as squeamish. The gunmaker made the barrel heavy to reduce the recoil and to ensure rigidity. Most were octagonal and fitted with sights and fired a fairly small diameter bullet.

It was in the design of the stock that much skill was expended, for the butt was made so that when the arm came up to fire, the pistol was on target almost without sighting. Stocks were rather hook-shaped and generally lacked all decoration except a little cross-hatching on the butt to afford a better grip. Triggers were often of the "set" type adjusted to operate with a minimum of pressure so that there should be no going off aim as the trigger was squeezed. Trigger guards often had a long spur to afford the first finger a good grip.

These pistols were usually supplied in pairs carefully fitted into a wooden case complete with accessories such as a bullet mould, screw driver, powder flask, cleaning rods and occasionally a mallet to tap home the tight-fitting bullet.

8   Read the following extract then write a summary of it in no more than 120 words.

The word "fan" is short for "fanatic" — and this means someone who is filled with excessive enthusiasm. A person in this state wants to see and read and hear everything he can about the sport or entertainment concerned — particularly about its stars. He just can't get enough of this material. He can stand having the same thing repeated over and over again. Therefore fan magazines have only been badly affected by television when the sport or entertainment itself has been badly affected. But the more football or pop music appears on television the more enthusiastic the fans become, and the keener they are to buy magazines about their idols.

Besides magazines for fans of a particular type of entertainment or sport, there are of course very special fan magazines about individual entertainers or groups. These are usually published by fan clubs for their members.

Fan magazines of all kinds are chiefly concerned with persons rather than things or ideas. For instance, a football fan magazine will carry far more articles about individual players than about the game itself — its laws, its competitions, its history, its management, its finances and so on. Similarly, a magazine for pop music fans will concentrate on individual stars and groups. There will be very little mention of such *technical* points as how pop songs are written or recorded, or of such *trade* details as how much it costs to build up a star's popularity, or how tours are planned and organised, or how publicity is arranged.

This doesn't mean that all articles about individual stars lack good solid information about the sport or entertainment concerned. A great many of them *are* trivial — mere "sucker-bait" as they are sometimes called. They do deal mainly with such non-technical details as what the star likes to eat or drink, how many suits he's got, what a success he is at parties, or how, for all his success, he's never forgotten the old folks back home. But some articles deal seriously with the star's attitude to his work, his methods of training, his opinions about the skill of other performers in the same job. And these can be very useful to people interested in the sport or profession for its own sake, and can also teach them something about the difficulties involved in being a star in any walk of life.

9   Write a summary of the following extract in about 70 words. You will not be able to include every item in the list of percentages but a statement of their overall signficance is needed.

Most packaging is unnecessary beyond the minimum required for health, safety and the reduction of damage to contents. The cost of reasonable packaging is obviously an advantage to both manufacturer and consumer, and the consumer is probably willing to pay the price.

However, are you aware of how much of the price is packaging and how much is the product? According to a survey by the trade magazine, *Modern Packaging*, an average of 18% of the retail price went into packaging costs. The percentage varied with the type of product and the type of container. Here are some of the results.

Table 1.   Percentage cost of packaging.

Paint in an aerosol can	16%
Paint in a conventional metal can	5%
Toy in a film-wrapped carton	14%
Toy mounted on a card, then sealed in plastic	8%
Motor oil in a metal can	26%
Small appliance in a corrugated carton	6%
Beer in a tinplate can	43%
Beer in a non-returnable glass bottle	36%

Frozen fish in a carton	5%
Moist petfood in a metal can	17%
Cereal in a folding carton	15%
Baby food in a glass jar	36%
Baby juice in a metal can	33%

Source: *Modern Packaging*, May 1967.

10 Write an outline in no more than 70 words of what can be learned about Charles Latimer Lewison from the following excerpt.

Charles Latimer Lewison described himself in *Who's Who* as an historian; and an historian he undoubtedly was. He had written books about the Hanseatic League, about the growth of banking in the seventeenth century and about the Gotha Programme of 1875, for example. He had been a university lecturer in England. He was the author of a biography of the eighteenth-century economist John Law considered by some to be the best work on the subject. Yet his reputation, outside a small segment of the academic world, rested in none of those achievements; it rested on the detective stories he wrote under the pseudonym of Charles Latimer. There were over twenty of these, and at least three — *A Bloody Shovel, Murder's Arms* and *No Doornail This* — had come to be regarded as classics in the genre. His work as an historian could only be read in English and had a limited appeal. His detective stories had been translated into many languages and had a worldwide appeal. They made not only his reputation as an entertainer but also the income on which he lived so comfortably in Majorca. When he disappeared they also made him news. As every reporter and most editorial writers hastened to point out, his disappearance was as mysterious and bizarre as one of his own novels.

Had he disappeared intentionally? If so, why and how?
Had he been abducted? If so, how and why?
Was he alive or dead?
Dead or alive, *where* was he?
Those were the questions the newspapers asked. Those, too, were the questions the police asked.

11 Read the extract that follows then write three paragraphs stating what you have learned about a) Benson Veteran Cycle Club (use about 30 words); b) Mr Ned Passey (about 50 words); c) the Benson Museum of Veteran and Vintage Cycles (about 60 words).

Daisy, riding down the golden Edwardian lanes on a Singer Safety Bicycle made for two, with her leg o'mutton sleeves and hems hooked on to her insteps to hide her bloomered ankles, would hardly be noticed if she cycled into Benson in Oxfordshire on a summer Sunday.

It would have to be the first Sunday in July, of course: the day of the annual rally of Benson Veteran Cycle Club. More that 200 cyclists gather in this comfortable village on which the local RAF aerodrome makes little impact. There isn't a bicycle later than 1925, not a hat that does not echo some sepia photograph, and the same sign up in Brook Street as in 1903: "B. Passey & Sons, Horse Slaughterers and Scrap Metal Merchants."

You can find Ned Passey, 53, horse slaughterer and founder of Benson Veteran Cycle Club, President of the National Association of Veteran and Vintage Cycle Clubs, and owner of 260 old bicycles, in an 80-guinea tweed knickerbocker suit sitting behind Mrs Passey on an 1892 Olympia Tandem Tricycle. Their daughter Muriel, 24, is on an 1867 crimson and white bone-shaker.

"The favourite of my collection, is this Olympia Tandem Tricycle," he says. "The wife persuaded an old man to sell it to her, after we married, and she'd got interested in bicycles too. . ."

Mrs Margaret Passey, ample in white bloomers, purple silk and flowered bonnet, demonstrates the tricycle.

"Handlebars come around from behind me, see — he sits behind."

"Ladies first, it always was," says Ned. "And see the little nose wheel at the front? Couldn't never tip up, this cycle, even when the gentleman got off at the back."

Ned Passey started collecting vintage cycles, made before 1914, 20 years ago, when he and three friends heard about a penny-farthing race from Ripley to Wandsworth.

"I'd got an old penny-farthing that was just laying about the place, and we got hold of a couple more and then someone else joined in and entered as well, and then we thought we'd start the club. We have 50 members now, all from within ten miles of Benson, and we keep it at that."

There are seven veteran and vintage cycle clubs in Britain, with membership rapidly growing as old bicycles are dug out of attics and farmyards.

"We had to include vintage cycles, to 1925," says Ned, "because so many people were finding the later ones."

Mr and Mrs Passey's Museum of Veteran and Vintage Cycles is housed at their bungalow in Benson, just across from the knacker's and scrap yard. It is a neat brick bungalow with a gnome each side of the polished front doorstep, and there is nothing to indicate what it conceals. But hundreds of visitors from as far as Japan, Holland and the USA discover it each year. And one step inside the front door is enough to become aware of bicycles. There are penny-farthings, bone-shakers, tandems and sociables on the walls, on mugs, ashtrays, clocks and candlesticks.

At the back of the bungalow is a large, green, corrugated iron hangar, and trimly massed within is the main part of the collection. In a nearby shed are piled penny-farthing tyres; more bicycles, old advertising signs, cycling accessories are stored along with Mrs Passey's orange brandy and marrow wine in the barn. In the attic of the bungalow is a sea of primed and polished cycle lamps ready for use.

"This is it," says Ned Passey, busily assembling bicycles and tricycles, bath-chairs and quadricycles, on the lawn; "we do use 'em all."

12 The following extract is about Houdini, the famous magician. Read it carefully then summarise a) the reasons why it seemed a good idea that Houdini should go into films, and b) the reasons why his films were failures. Your whole answer should not exceed 65 words.

Houdini's decision to appear in films was warmly welcomed in the trade. He could bring to the new industry a famous name, an enthusiastic public, and a talent for thrilling escapes which ought — producers believed — to be well-adapted to the medium of motion pictures. Apparently it occurred to no-one, least of all to Houdini, that acting ability might also be a requirement for success. In 1919 he made his first picture, a serial called "The Master Mystery", which was followed by two others, "The Grim Game" and "Terror Island". All utilized Houdini's best-known skills to the utmost: the stories were so devised that he was called upon to escape — and rescue the heroine — from every conceivable type of restraint, to slide down cliffs, to leap from one airplane to another in mid-air, to fight under water, and — of course — inevitably to defeat the villain. Houdini actually performed all the stunts shown on the screen, and he was injured more than once during the course of his work.

Unfortunately for him, however, many movie heroes were

performing on the screen stunts which looked quite as dangerous as Houdini's — clever photography had already been accepted as an adequate substitute for courage. All of them could be made to *appear* to leap from one plane to another, although they may never have been more than a foot or two off the ground. And many of their performances were doubly effective because they were given by gifted actors, men able to imbue their scenes with reality, to portray tenderness and passion as well as extraordinary skill and strength.

It was only the last of these qualities that Houdini brought to his screen performances. He regarded the always-present heroine as a waste of screen footage, and his necessary scenes with her as useless interludes between stirring episodes of escape. The inevitable result was that the public, despite its admiration for Houdini's stage performances, refused to admire him as a screen hero. He wasn't, in the movies' own phrase, "the type".

13 The following observations were made by schoolchildren about teachers. Write a report in no more than 100 words summarising the main points which are made.

The teachers, especially head teachers, should be nearer the age of the children, especially in secondary schools. If they were, they would be able to understand our point of view, why we disagree with their opinions on rules, uniform, etc, and not just say: "Don't be insolent, take a detention."

Gillian, 13

Respect for the pupil is just as important as respect for the teacher, because after a young person's opinion has been disregarded three or four times the young person may never express an opinion again.

Sheila, 15

Teachers I think should have extra training to be able to control a class. I know we teenagers can be really spiteful, but I think it is partly the teacher's fault. If he or she had a certain amount of discipline, there would not be so many riots as there are in our school. I think if a teacher cannot control a class, the teacher should either give the job up, go away for disciplinary training, or become a nervous wreck.

Rachel, 15

Teachers would have to be punctual for lessons. Sometimes a whole lesson is wasted because a teacher is late.

Janet, 14

The school I would like is one where there are young teachers, because I find that most teachers who have been teaching for a long time try to model schools on what it was like in their own schooldays when it was not as enjoyable as today.

Mark, 12

The staff would go on a compulsory course every five years to ensure that they know about the latest developments in both education generally and their own subjects.

Janice, 16

. . . teachers that were old-fashioned should be got rid of. Old-fashioned teachers are the type that give out lines to a class that makes the slightest noise; they also regard the pupils' opinions as cheek.

Ruth, 13

Teachers should be more enthusiastic about their subject. There is nothing worse than sitting in a lesson knowing full well that the teacher is dying to get rid of you and rush back to the staff-room to have her cup of tea.

Ruth, 15

The staff would have to be prepared not to leave in the middle of the year, as they seem to — at least, in my present school.

Janet, 16

I know one thing that I would make a rule, it's to have all the teachers meet our mothers at school, only if it's once a term it would be the best thing which ever happened.

K. (boy), 13

14 Summarise in about 70 words what you have learned about Mr Slope from the following extract.

Mr Slope is tall and not ill made. His feet and hands are large, as has ever been the case with all his family, but he has a broad chest and wide shoulders to carry off these excrescences, and on the whole his figure is good. His countenance, however, is not specially prepossessing. His hair is lank, and of a dull pale reddish hue. It is always formed into three straight lumpy masses, each brushed with admirable precision, and cemented with much grease; two of them adhere closely to the sides of his face, and the other lies at right angles above them. He wears no whiskers, and is always punctiliously shaven. His face is nearly of the same colour as his hair, though perhaps a little redder; it is not unlike beef — beef, however, one would say, of a bad quality. His forehead is capacious and high, but square and heavy, and unpleasantly shining. His mouth is large, though his lips are thin and bloodless; and his big, prominent, pale brown eyes inspire anything but confidence. His nose, however, is his redeeming feature: it is pronounced straight and well-formed; though I myself should have liked it better did it not possess a somewhat spongy, porous appearance, as though it had been cleverly formed out of a red coloured cork.

I could never endure to shake hands with Mr Slope. A cold, clammy perspiration always exudes from him, the small drops are ever to be seen standing on his brow, and his friendly grasp is unpleasant.

15 The passage that follows takes a look into the future. Summarise what it has to say about a) education (max. words 70) and b) housing (max. words 30).

We might imagine a classroom around the year 2000, where each of 200 students has his or her own television screen and personal controls that allow the running through of the lesson-film at the rate that best suits the individual: a lesson-film that could include or skip repeats and more detailed information. In such a classroom, the human lecturer would spend, say, half-hour periods with small seminar groups of not more than ten or a dozen students at a time, answering their questions and planning the written work they would do on the subjects in their "homework" or "private study" period.

This sort of teaching method, although unsuitable for the smallest children, who need the mother-like reality of talking to and even touching their teacher (as many a bruised infant-school instructress can testify), would probably work efficiently for normal children from eight years old upwards and also for adults, for whom such methods are even now being used for the Open University.

This machine aid would make education less expensive to the state, and less expense, in turn, would mean that people might take a longer time to absorb academic knowledge, interspersing such study with manual skills and creative work or doing practical work in their particular field. Primary schools would probably be most usefully sited within individual communities, near to children's homes, but senior schools and universities might form part of a centre-city or intercommunity complex where a group of buildings of particular social and architectural interest might make a focal point for civic pride and sightseeing. Such a centre could also include fountains, gardens and cafés, where people could go to sit out — on the pavements, when the climate was right, or else under transparent domes to watch the world go by. Other buildings in this type of area might include an art gallery, a library, a museum, theatres for professional and amateur dramatic performances, cinemas, skating-rinks, civic offices and meeting halls.

Houses in a Creative Society, however varied in plan and architectural style, would have as a common factor that each would be large enough to allow every member of the household to have space to indulge his or her hobby; which would probably, of course, include gardening, so that streets might be brightened by flowering trees and climbing plants trailing over garden walls or down from apartment roof-gardens. No block of apartments, however, would be more than four storeys high and outlying neighbourhoods would be saved from drab, dead-end suburban uniformity by being interspersed with their own service buildings such as shops, schools, craft centres, dance and meeting halls, swimming baths and perhaps even the occasional office block. Above all these buildings, the parks, the streets, the squares, would run a noiseless monorail, graceful and glittering on high columns, linking streets at half-mile intervals with community focal points or city centres.

16   Read carefully this extract from a play and then summarise in about 150 words all the arguments used by Mr Browne to persuade the Inspector that he should not attempt to open the cellar door.

(The scene is the study of Callingham Manor.)

Inspector: We've searched the whole house and grounds but there's no sign of your wife. You're sure there aren't any hidden rooms or anything?

Mr Browne: Quite sure.

Inspector: What about a cellar? I'm surprised a house this size and age hasn't got one.

Mr Browne: There's none that I know of.

Inspector: Where does that door to the right of the kitchen lead?

Mr Browne: I didn't realise there was a door there. I hardly ever go into the servants' quarters.

Inspector: Well, I'd like you to look now if you don't mind.

Mr Browne: Actually, it's not convenient at the moment. I've an appointment to see my solicitor in Bewley at three.

Inspector: This won't take a minute. I'd be glad if you'd follow me.

Mr Browne: Very well. But it's a waste of time. I showed you right round the house when I first reported my wife was missing.

(They go out of the study in the direction of the servants' quarters.)

Inspector: This is the door I meant, sir.

Mr Browne: Oh, that one — I'd forgotten it existed.

Inspector: It seems to be locked.

Mr Browne: Yes. I remember now that the man from the house agents said the key was lost.

Inspector: But surely you've been curious to know where the door leads?

Mr Browne: Not really. The house is big enough as it is and none of us drinks wine so we've never felt the need for a cellar.

Inspector: Wouldn't it be useful for storing other things?

Mr Browne: We have plenty of storage space. You've seen the attics, haven't you?

Inspector: Yes, sir, I have seen *them*. And I'd very much like to see what's behind this door.

Mr Browne: I can assure you that it's never been open since we moved in here last November.

Inspector: Maybe — but I'd still like to satisfy my curiosity. Perhaps your wife found the key, went exploring and got shut in?

Mr Browne: Don't be preposterous. She never does anything without telling me.

Inspector: I wouldn't be too sure of that. Women get some strange notions sometimes.

Mr Browne: Well, Muriel wouldn't do anything like that. She has a highly nervous disposition and when the cook told us this end of the house is haunted, she wanted to move out straightaway. She would never have come here on her own.

Inspector: You didn't mention that in your statement, sir.

Mr Browne: It didn't seem important.

Inspector: To go back to the door — I'd like to open it up.

Mr Browne: I'm not having anyone breaking down doors. It's cost a fortune to renovate this place already.

Inspector: No question of breaking and entering, sir. I'll get a specialist to pick the lock.

Mr Browne: I'm afraid that won't be possible. It's a medieval lock and hasn't been touched for centuries.

Inspector: No problem. We have our methods.

Mr Browne: I don't think you have the legal right. I'll speak to my solicitor about it.

Inspector: It's my duty to take all the steps necessary to trace your wife and that includes blasting in that door if we have to.

Mr Browne: You sound like someone in the IRA — not a responsible police officer. Your job is to protect property, not to smash it up.

Inspector: I'm afraid a human life comes before property, sir. I'll be back at 10.30 tomorrow morning with a locksmith and I must insist that this door is opened.

Mr Browne: That won't be possible. I'm going down to the West Country tonight and the servants have been given a few days off. If you insist, it'll have to be some time next week.

Inspector: Very well. Tomorrow week at 10.30. Unless, of course, Mrs Browne has been found by then. The whole force is on the alert.

Mr Browne: I understand.

Inspector: Don't worry. I'll see myself out.

(As soon as the Inspector has gone, Mr Browne takes a large iron key from the back pocket of his trousers and proceeds to unlock the cellar door . . .)

17 Write a summary of the passage that follows in no more than 120 words.

We live now in what can be called a drug-taking culture. By that I mean taking drugs is a common aspect of our everyday lives. Look how we advertise them on television, in our magazines and on the sides of our buses. Whenever we have a headache, or feel sick or tired, or have eaten indiscriminately, we are exhorted that somewhere there is a tablet that will bring us immediate relief.

Go into your bathroom and look into the cabinet; what do you find? The ubiquitous aspirin and codeine, antiseptics like Dettol or T.C.P., some antibiotics for that bad attack of bronchitis, some sleeping pills, last year's tonic, some cough mixture, perhaps the contraceptive pill, even some anti-depressants forgotten in a corner.

Look in your bedroom and you will find some beauty

preparations with hormones to promote the illusions of perpetual youth.

Look in the garage and you will find insecticides and artificial fertilisers.

Look in the living-room and you will find tea, coffee and cocoa, all of which contain caffeine; the cigarettes, cigars and pipe tobacco that contain nicotine; the spirits, wines and beers in the cupboard that contain alcohol.

We are surrounded by drugs in our own homes; we are all drug users, but most of us do not abuse or misuse drugs except on the rare occasion of a party or the evening out.

Our children are brought up in a world in which they see us, the adults, turn to drugs for relief, comfort and stimulation, and when they grow up it is little surprise that they take to drugs in their turn. What is surprising to them, and considered to be hypocritical, is the indignation of the adult world when youth copies age. There is certainly a problem of drug misuse in young people, but there is equally a problem of drug misuse in older people but it is not talked about and does not hit the headlines because it is not sensational — the middle aged who are dependent on barbiturates to get off to sleep, on appetite suppressants to get their weight down but excite like amphetamines, and on tranquillisers to control the crippling anxiety which would stop them getting through another day.

Drugs are very much a part of modern life; drugs are available, and so drugs are used, and because of human weaknesses, misused.

18   The following extract is taken from *Alive*, a true account of a plane crash in the Andes involving a Uruguayan rugby team and its supporters. Summarise in no more than 100 words the reasons why it was inevitable that the survivors would have to take the advice of one of their number, Canessa, a medical student.

Starvation was taking its effect. They were becoming weaker and more listless. When they stood up they felt faint and found it difficult to keep their balance. They felt cold, even when the sun rose to warm them, and their skin started to grow wrinkled like that of old men.

Their food supplies were running out. The daily ration of a scrap of chocolate, a capful* of wine, and a teaspoonful of

* The cap was from a salvaged container.

jam or tinned fish — eaten slowly to make it last — was more torture than sustenance for these healthy athletic boys; yet the strong shared it with the weak, the healthy with the injured. It was clear to them all that they could not survive much longer. It was not so much that they were consumed with ravenous hunger as that they felt themselves grow weaker each day, and no knowledge of medicine or nutrition was required to predict how it would end.

Their minds turned to other sources of food. It seemed impossible that there should be nothing whatsoever growing in the Andes, for even the meanest form of plant life might provide some nutrition. In the immediate vicinity of the plane there was only snow. The nearest soil was a hundred feet below them. The only ground exposed to sun and air was barren mountain rock on which they found nothing but brittle lichen. They scraped some of it off and mixed it into a paste with melted snow, but the taste was bitter and disgusting, and as food it was worthless. Except for the lichens there was nothing. Some thought of the cushions, but even these were not stuffed with straw. Nylon and foam rubber would not help them.

For some days several of the boys had realized that if they were to survive they would have to eat the bodies of those who had died in the crash. It was a ghastly prospect. The corpses lay around the plane in the snow, preserved by the intense cold in the state in which they had died. While the thought of cutting flesh from those who had been their friends was deeply repugnant to them all, a lucid appreciation of their predicament led them to consider it.

Gradually the discussion spread as these boys cautiously mentioned it to their friends or to those they thought would be sympathetic. Finally, Canessa brought it out into the open. He argued forcibly that they were not going to be rescued; that they would have to escape themselves, but that nothing could be done without food; and that the only food was human flesh. He used his knowledge of medicine to describe, in his penetrating, high-pitched voice, how their bodies were using up their reserves. "Every time you move," he said, "you use up part of your own body. Soon we shall be so weak that we won't have the strength even to cut the meat that is lying there before our eyes."

Canessa did not argue just from expediency. He insisted that they had a moral duty to stay alive by any means at their disposal, and because Canessa was earnest about his religious belief, great weight was given to what he said by the more pious among the survivors.

"It is meat," he said. "That's all it is. The souls have left their bodies and are in heaven with God. All that is left here are the carcases, which are no more human beings than the dead flesh of the cattle we eat at home."

Others joined in the discussion. "Didn't you see," said Fito Strauch, "how much energy we needed just to climb a few hundred feet up the mountain? Think how much more we'll need to climb to the top and then down the other side. It can't be done on a sip of wine and a scrap of chocolate."

The truth of what he said was incontestable.

19 The following points were made during a discussion on euthanasia (mercy-killing). Using only the opinions presented here, write a summary of a) the case *for* euthanasia (max. 80 words) and b) the case *against* (max. 60 words).

No one has the right to take the life of another.
The drugs bill could be slashed if incurables were "put to sleep".
An individual over 70 should be able to choose death rather than pain.
Our resources should be spent on the living not the half-dead.
Doctors do not want the responsibility of deciding whether a person should be allowed to die.
The strong should not have to carry the weak.
It is worth prolonging life as a cure for that particular illness might be discovered.
The Bible says "Thou shalt not kill".
What is the point of being kept alive in a permanent coma?
In the wrong hands euthanasia can be a dangerous political weapon (Hitler and the Jews).
A mother should have the right to decide that her severely handicapped child's life should be terminated.
Euthanasia is legalised murder.
People kept alive on kidney machines etc. are not leading a natural life. They should be allowed to die.
You can't choose whether you are born weak or strong.
It is not economic to prolong life artificially.
Life as a "cabbage" is worse than death.
Euthanasia should be permitted in cases of severe mental illness only.
Eliminating inferior physical specimens would improve the race.
Mercy-killing is the next logical step after legalised abortion.

20 Read the following dialogue then a) summarise in one paragraph the arguments used by Ken to persuade his mother to let him go to the party, and b) in a second paragraph summarise his mother's objections to his going. Use no more than 75 words in each paragraph.

Ken: Mum, can I go to Keith's party on Saturday?

Mum: Why? You're always out at parties. We never see you these days — only for meals.

Ken: Well, this one's a bit special — it's his sixteenth birthday. He's hiring the Youth Club hall and having a group.

Mum: I wouldn't listen to that racket if you paid me. You'll all be deaf before you're twenty-one.

Ken: There'll be food and plenty to drink . . .

Mum: And that's another thing. What's this I hear about you being in The Rose and Crown last Friday night? Drinking beer from what I'm told. I expect you're looking forward to getting drunk at Keith's party.

Ken: Don't be silly. All I ever drink is shandy and you can't get drunk on that.

Mum: I wouldn't be too sure. Some of your so-called mates like Mick Field are quite capable of mixing in something strong. I suppose he'll be there?

Ken: There's nothing wrong with Mick. Just because he was unlucky in that car and the police caught him.

Mum: I don't see that driving under age, without a licence and with no insurance. . .

Ken: All right, all right. We've heard all that before. Danny's going to give me a lift anyway.

Mum: But I thought he'd smashed up his mother's car.

Ken: No. He got run into by some woman at the traffic lights, that's all.

Mum: What sort of a driver is he?

Ken: Very steady. He passed his test at the first go.

Mum: And what time do you expect to be back? I don't want you making a noise half-way through the night. Your father's got to get up early for work the next morning. Remember the last time you all came in for a quiet coffee.

Ken: That was Raymond Bax's fault and he's not going on Saturday. I admit he's a bit wild.

Mum: And what about girls? You know I don't like that crowd that hangs around the club. I should have thought you'd had enough of that Maureen Blakey.

Ken:	Oh come on. That's ancient history. Anyway, she won't be there. There'll be no gate-crashers. Keith's only having his friends and there'll be somebody on the door to keep out 'undesirables' as you would call them.
Mum:	Well, I don't know. You're supposed to be going over to Aunt Edna's early on Sunday morning to help move that shed.
Ken:	Oh I'd forgotten about that. I reckon I could still get across for nine.
Mum:	Some hopes. I can't see you getting up at eight after a party.
Ken:	You'll see. A bit of exercise will help to clear my head.
Mum:	After all that smoke I suppose — not to mention the drink.
Ken:	I'm beginning to be sorry I mentioned it. I suppose I should stay in for a thrilling evening watching you and Dad go to sleep watching the telly.
Mum:	There's no need to be rude. Your Dad likes to relax quietly after a hard day. Pity you don't do a bit more school work in the evenings instead of going out so much.
Ken:	I'm staying in tonight and tomorrow night to get up to date before the weekend. . . Can I go on Saturday?
Mum:	Well, ask your Dad when he comes in.
Ken:	Thanks, Mum.

CRITICAL ANALYSIS

21 Read the following extract carefully. It is a passage for précis set by one of the GCE Examination Boards in an O-level paper. It contains 347 words and has to be reduced to 120. Notice the general theme and consider what points you would include in a summary of it.

Looking beyond our lifetime at modes of transport should be an interesting exercise. Predictions tend to be based on known technology and current fashion. The Victorians thought that the skies of the twentieth century would be darkened by steam-driven balloons manned by gentlemen in top hats. The thirties idea of the airliner of the future was an enormous aeroplane powered by a score or more propellers.

Only the immediate future can be viewed with a reasonable certainty of what will happen.

A look backwards demonstrates how rapid are the changes. A hundred years ago there were no motor cars, no aircraft, no electrically powered trains and trams: but it seemed then a wondrous era. Thanks to steam, man could roam the seas at will, or reach the furthermost corner of the country from London in a matter of hours. Someone aged fifty in 1872 was born three years before the first railway, in an age when man was still dependent on animal and wind-power. But if that same Victorian had lived on for another fifty years he would have seen changes that would have made 1872 look like the Dark Ages. By 1922 the whole of Greater London was covered by a network of tramways and motor bus routes. Underground electric trains carried commuters to distant suburbs. Private cars had superseded the horse. It was possible to fly to Paris, but most overseas travellers voyaged on ocean liners in unexcelled comfort. Those people of 1922 would have found it hard to believe that those same liners would be made obsolete by jet airliners. They would have regarded it as incomprehensible that the efficient British trams would become as extinct as dinosaurs, and they certainly would have had difficulty in accepting that men actually would go to the Moon.

So there are no holds barred when it comes to looking a hundred years ahead. In the intervening time there are many discoveries to be made, new technologies to be applied, new energy sources to replace those that are running out or are too damaging environmentally to be further exploited.

Now look in turn at these four attempts at summarising the passage. They were produced by students following an O level course and they are unsatisfactory for a variety of reasons. Decide in what ways each one is inadequate and then discuss your findings with your teacher and others in your group. Particular faults to look for are inaccurate statements, omission of important ideas, copying verbatim from the passage, adding of ideas not in the original and the inclusion of lists. These are all likely to occur in précis-writing but you may also find other more general faults such as jerky style and bad grammar.

Remember that constructive criticism is more valuable than destructive and that it's easy to criticise other people's work. What you must do in the weeks ahead is to be increasingly critical of your own efforts.

Attempt A   Predictions of what might happen tend to be based on known technology and current fashion. Only the immediate future can be viewed with a reasonable certainty of what will happen. From 1872 to 1922 rapid changes went on. In 1872 man was dependent on steam for transport but only 50 years later in 1922 Greater London was filled with networks for trams, underground services and buses. Some people even owned their own car. We cannot forecast the future with any certainty. From now and into the future many discoveries have yet to be made, new energy sources to replace those that are running out or are too damaging environmentally to be further exploited.

(113 words)

Attempt B   During the Victorian era people wondered what sort of transport would be used during the years to come. They imagined that we would still be riding in hot air balloons. A hundred years ago there were no cars, aircraft or trains but as time evolved more and more time-saving modes of transport were invented. Now there is no holding men back. Machines are made faster and faster, ships and planes have special gadgets to hold more people and men are now actually flying to the moon. As with the new inventions, new sources of energy have to be found. North Sea gas, special electric batteries, nuclear energy are all comparatively new discoveries.

(112 words)

Attempt C   Looking forward in time can be very interesting though we tend to base predictions on known fact. And only the immediate future can be predicted with reasonable certainty. One hundred years ago there was none of the modern means of transport we know today. People were dependent on animals for transport. Fifty years later London had a network of public transport. Within another fifty years the use of steam was only for nostalgia. Between now and another hundred years many things will be discovered to change everyday life. New sources of energy will replace those run out and too damaging environmentally to carry on.

(104 words)

Attempt D   Safe predictions on future transport are based on known technology and current fashion. Only the immediate future can be foreseen with certainty. Vehicles of today were not seen 100 years ago. Steam has made fast travelling possible. A man born in 1872 would find changes 50 years later hard to accept. By 1922 Greater London was

covered by a network of tramways, bus routes and underground trains were in use. Private cars have replaced horses
and ocean liners are now replaced by jet airliners. These
people would not be able to believe that trams are extinct
and men go to the moon. Finally, in future years many
discoveries will be made in the way of energy sources and
technology.

(119 words)

22 Write a summary of the following extract in no more than
120 words. State at the end the number of words that you have
used.

Many lurid and blood-curdling tales have been told about
sharks. At the risk of incurring the wrath of sensational
journalists and the more unscrupulous naturalists it must be
said at once that most of these are without foundation.
Although carnivorous in habit, sharks are in general harmless
to man. Their reputation as man-eaters is based on very few
well-authenticated cases, and they are only really dangerous
when there is a scent of blood in the water. This arouses in
them the same lust to kill as a retreating fox inspires in the
more moronic members of the human species, and it is then
advisable to give them a wide berth. In normal circumstances,
however, the shark is a peaceable member of the ocean
community whose only wish is to be left to mind his own
business while others mind theirs.

The limited numbers of substantiated attacks on human
beings have mainly been the work of one species, the great
white shark. This is found in all the warm seas of the world,
and is an occasional visitor to temperate waters. The average
length of the animal is between twenty and forty feet, but
much larger specimens are known to exist. Thus some white
shark teeth dredged from the floor of the Pacific during the
famous *Challenger* expedition of the last century measured
no less than five inches long. By comparison with the teeth of
specimens whose length is known, it can be deduced that the
owner of these teeth must have measured at least seventy feet
from nose to tail.

The animal is exceptionally voracious, and many kinds of
fish and even young sea lions form part of its diet. It not only
takes living prey, but is also a scavenger, feeding on the refuse
and offal discharged from ships in harbour. The stomach of
one great white shark was found to contain a tin can, a

number of mutton bones, the hind quarters of a pig, the head
and fore-quarters of a bulldog, and a quantity of horseflesh;
another had consumed a large Newfoundland dog ("with his
collar on", the report adds). Such animals, even though their
attacks on human beings may be rare, are to be discouraged
near bathing places.

23 Write a summary of the following extract in no more than
120 words. State at the end the number you have used.

The Englishman's home today is not his castle. It is his
centrally-heated, clean, bright, combined nesting-cage and
exercise-run. The family-size television set replaces the
crowded cinema, the bottle of beer from the off-licence the
visit to the pub, the telly discussion the pub argument.
Furnishing and decorating the home have become subjects of
absorbing interest to the nation while public architecture has
degenerated into a featureless bore.

The homes we live in cater for this stay-at-home, stay-
separated trend. The tall flats discourage neighbourliness.
Nobody passes by your window on the tenth floor. You are
too far away from life there to exchange shouted greetings or
gather material for gossip by keen observation of neighbours'
comings and goings. In the flats there are no garden fences to
gossip over and the vestibules of the blocks have a forbidding
air which discourages social loitering.

Even more discouraging to the maintenance of day-to-day
links with the outside world are the estates of council semis
stretching for miles around the outskirts of cities. To go to
town means a long walk in the rain, perhaps a long wait for
an uncertain bus or a trip in the car to struggle for a parking
place — none of them inviting prospects. An allotment near
the semi satisfies the need for fresh air, exercise and
communing with nature.

Of course the managers of the human factory-farms must
see to it that their charges thrive. While animals' needs are
imperfectly understood, it is well known that humans, at
least, need an occasional change. So the car becomes a mobile
home, bearing separate individually packaged families on a
bitumen or concrete conveyor-belt to the seaside. Once a
year consumers are gathered from the nesting-boxes and
broilerhouses of Sheffield, Liverpool and London, packed
into aircraft and efficiently transported to concrete nesting-
boxes on the Mediterranean coasts in resorts which were once

places of peace and beauty and are now extensions of
industrial Europe's human chicken-run.

24 Read these extracts from the autobiography of Charles
Chaplin then sum up the character and 'atmosphere' of
a) London; b) Paris; c) New York as described here. Be careful
to use your own words and do not exceed 110 altogether.

London was sedate in those days. The tempo was sedate;
even the horse-drawn tram-cars along Westminster Bridge
Road went at a sedate pace and turned sedately on a revolving
table at the terminal near the bridge. In Mother's prosperous
days we also lived in Westminster Bridge Road. Its atmosphere
was gay and friendly with attractive shops, restaurants and
music halls. The fruit-shop on the corner facing the Bridge
was a galaxy of colour, with its neatly arranged pyramids of
oranges, apples, pears and bananas outside, in contrast to the
solemn grey Houses of Parliament directly across the river.
 This was the London of my childhood, of my moods and
awakenings: memories of Lambeth in the spring; of trivial
incidents and things; of riding with Mother on top of a horse-
bus trying to touch passing lilac trees — of the many coloured
bus tickets, orange, blue, pink and green, that bestrewed the
pavement where the trams and buses stopped — of rubicund
flower-girls at the corner of Westminster Bridge, making gay
boutonnières, their adroit fingers manipulating tinsel and
glittering fern — of the humid odour of freshly watered roses
that affected me with a vague sadness — of melancholy
Sundays and pale-faced parents and their children escorting
toy windmills and coloured balloons over Westminster Bridge
and the maternal penny steamers that softly lowered their
funnels as they glided under it. From such trivia I believe my
soul was born.

*　　*　　*

It was late autumn and the journey from Calais to Paris was
dreary. Nevertheless, as we neared Paris my excitement grew.
We had passed through bleak, lonely country. Then gradually
out of the darkened sky we saw an illumination. "That", said
a Frenchman in the carriage with us, "is the reflection of
Paris."
 Paris was everything I expected. The drive from the Gare
du Nord to the rue Geoffroy-Marie had me excited and
impatient; I wanted to stop at every corner and walk. It was
seven in the evening; the golden lights shone invitingly from

the cafés and their outside tables spoke of an enjoyment of
life. But for the innovation of a few motor-cars, it was still
the Paris of Monet, Pissarro and Renoir. It was Sunday and
everyone seemed pleasure-bent. Gaiety and vitality were in
the air. Even my room in the rue Geoffroy-Marie, with its
stone floor, which I called my Bastille, could not dampen my
ardour, for one lived sitting at tables outside bistros and
cafés.

*   *   *

I was alien to this slick tempo. In New York even the owner
of the smallest enterprise acts with alacrity. The shoe-black
flips his polishing rag with alacrity, the bartender serves a
beer with alacrity, sliding it up to you along the polished
surface of the bar. The soda-clerk, when serving an egg malted
milk, performs like a hopped-up juggler. In a fury of speed he
snatches up a glass, attacking everything he puts into it,
vanilla flavour, blob of ice-cream, two spoonfuls of malt, a
raw egg which he deposits with one crack, then adding milk,
all of which he shakes in a container and delivers in less than
a minute.

On the Avenue that first day many looked as I felt, lone
and isolated; others swaggered along as though they owned
the place. The behaviour of many people seemed dour and
metallic as if to be agreeable or polite would prove a weakness.
But in the evening as I walked along Broadway with the
crowd dressed in their summer clothes, I became reassured.
We had left England in the middle of a bitter cold September
and arrived in New York in an Indian summer with a temper-
ature of eighty degrees; and as I walked along Broadway it
began to light up with myriads of coloured electric bulbs and
sparkled like a brilliant jewel. And in the warm night my
attitude changed and the meaning of America came to me:
the tall sky-scrapers, the brilliant, gay lights, the thrilling
display of advertisements stirred me with hope and a sense of
adventure. "That is it!" I said to myself. "This is where I
belong!"

25   Read this account from the *Daily Herald* newspaper of the
sinking of the *Titanic* then write a summary in three paragraphs
covering a) why and how the ship sank; b) the rescue of some of
the passengers; c) allegations of preferential treatment for First
Class passengers. Your whole summary should not exceed 150
words and you must state at the end the number you have used.

GRIM STORIES FROM THE TITANIC'S SURVIVORS
Indescribable Suffering in the Boats

. . . Mr C.H. Stengel, a first-class passenger, said that when the *Titanic* struck the iceberg the impact was terrific, and great blocks of ice were thrown on the deck, killing a number of people. The stern of the vessel rose in the air, and people ran shrieking from their berths below. Women and children, some of the former naturally hysterical, having been rapidly separated from husbands, brothers and fathers, were quickly placed in boats by the sailors, who like their officers, it was stated, were heard by some survivors to threaten men that they would shoot if male passengers attempted to get in the boats ahead of the women. Indeed, it was said that shots were actually heard. Mr Stengel added that a number of men threw themselves into the sea when they saw that there was no chance of reaching the boats. "How they died", he observed, "I do not know." He dropped overboard, caught hold of the gunwhale of a boat, and was pulled in because there were not enough sailors to handle her. In some of the boats women were shrieking for their husbands; others were weeping, but many bravely took a turn at the oars.

Mrs Bonnell, of Youngstown, Ohio, said the *Titanic* was ploughing through icefields when the collision occurred. A large proportion of the passengers were asleep. The bottom bow drove into the iceberg and the lower plates were torn asunder. Large volumes of water rushed in with irresistible force, and the liner began to sink rapidly by the bow. The *Titanic* seemed to slide across the top of the berg. The passengers hurriedly seized their clothing, and immediately the lifeboats were made ready. As the liner continued to gradually recede into the trough of the sea the passengers marched towards the stern. The orchestra belonging to the first class assembled on deck as the liner was going down and played "Nearer My God to Thee".

By that time most of the lifeboats were some distance away, and only a faint sound of the strains of the hymn could be heard as we pulled away from the ship. We noticed that she was hog-backed, showing that she was already breaking in two. She was not telescoped, the force of the impact being sustained in the keel more than the bows. We were in the small boats for more than four hours before we were rescued by the *Carpathia*. There were icefields and icefloes all around us. They were constantly grinding and washing together, and the boats were in danger of being dashed to pieces. The weather was extremely cold, and we suffered intensely. The men on the boats showed splendid heroism. There was no panic among the steerage or second-class passengers, though it was alleged that there was a wild scramble among the first-class passengers and I am informed that shots were fired. We were all cared for on board the *Carpathia* and shown every courtesy and kindness. The mental condition of all was good, considering the terrible ordeal, until the *Carpathia* reached New York Bay, but then there were numerous cases of collapse and mental derangements. . .

FIRST-CLASS FIRST
Class Discrimination on the 'Titanic'

The various representatives of the capitalist Press have taken Mr Ben Tillett sharply to task for declaring, in a printed statement, that obvious discrimination was apparent in favour of the cabin passengers when the *Titanic*'s lifeboats were being manned. Mr Tillett probably overstated himself when he spoke of "the vicious class antagonism shown in the practical forbidding of the saving of the lives of the third-class passengers."

That the facts in the long run justify Mr Tillett, however, is shown in the proportions of those rescued in each class to their several totals, which the *Daily Herald* here prints for the first time. They are as follows:

	Per cent
Proportion of 1st Class saved	61
Proportion of 2nd Class saved	36
Proportion of 3rd Class saved	23
Proportion of Crew saved	22
Proportion of whole Ship's Company	29

26 Write a summary of the following passage in no more than 140 words. State at the end the number of words that you have used.

We went to the sea-side every summer. A change of air was considered a good thing, especially the ozone we inhaled from the sea air and sea weed. Very diligently, mother went searching for pleasant beaches and good accommodation for us. This was not such an undertaking then as it is today for the roads were comparatively free from traffic; there were far fewer bodies about which made travelling easier. And at least there was always room and to spare on our lovely beaches and accommodation did not have to be booked months ahead. In this respect we were luckier than some because our parents always rented a whole house, which I suppose was reasonable with our sized family. And as we took the cook and a maid in addition to the nursery staff, what could be simpler?

The modern child, blasé and bored as country after country flashes by beneath its nose as the jets roar across the world, could never understand what excitement we enjoyed when our trunks were brought out to be packed for our little train journey; for us it was a truly great adventure.

A whole first class carriage was reserved for us, but before we could entrain an important "ceremony" took place. The footman was sent ahead to disinfect it. Behold, therefore, William or Alfred or whomsoever, having first carefully shut all the windows, directing with determination and thoroughness his spray of formalin all over the upholstery and especially into the many dirty little corners in which a germ might be lying in wait for us. His task accomplished, I suppose he aired the carriage before we arrived. I wonder what the station-master and porters thought of such goings on?

Mother usually went on ahead with cook or housemaid to get the house and beds properly aired. Nannie followed with us and nursery maid or governess or both, the following day. Mother insisted on such a regular routine that nothing, not even a train journey, was allowed to break it. We ate our lunch in the carriage but in a less conventional way than usual. Cold chicken we held in our fingers (previously sponged and dried by our nurserymaid), cold rice pudding dug out of the enamel dish with our spoons with cold apple purée from a glass jar with a screwed-on top. After that, we stretched out on the seats on rugs for our usual rest.

One event of which I did not approve was when nannie opened the round tin footbath which had a lid and was firmly strapped down and which was filled to the brim with Francis's nappies and the potty and probably other things as well. Nannie pulled the blinds down while Francis sat on his pot, after which performance she opened the window and emptied it onto the track. I could never understand how nannie could possibly have known if the next-door carriage windows were closed.

27 This passage describes the Victory March after the First World War. It took place in London on July 19th 1919. Read the account carefully then write a summary in three paragraphs covering a) the Victory March itself; b) the celebrations in London that same evening; c) the problems faced by the officers and men demobilised from the services. Your whole summary must not exceed 160 words and the number used should be stated.

It was a magnificent pageant of the fighting men of all branches in the Army, and of naval men from the Grand Fleet, and airmen and merchant seamen, and women from the services. One forgot for a little while the troubled state of Europe, the low-grade morality of European statesmen, the land-grabbing already happening, the failure to make 'homes for heroes', or to redeem any of the promises held out to the nation. This was our Victory Day, and a tribute by vast crowds to those who had saved us in time of war. There were many men in the crowd who still wore hospital blue, and many — given front places — who had wheeled themselves here in chairs for cripples. One watched the passing of this pageant with emotion. These men marching by were those whom I had seen covered with the clay of Flanders and the white chalk of the Somme. Now for an hour or two they had their reward. They were the heroes. They deserved the roaring cheers of the crowd, rising louder, as I was glad to hear, when our merchant seamen — neglected before the war and forgotten afterwards — went by with unmartial step. We owed our victory, our liberty, our lives, to all of these. The old, old Past walked with them — all our history and all our ghosts.

That night London went mad, but the most part of it was a decent joyous madness without vice in it. I was caught up in the surging crowds who linked arms and were cheering and singing. Outside Buckingham Palace they called for the King time and time again, and he had to come out to his balcony, with the Queen and his family, smiling down on this vast multitude, raising his hand to them. At night I found myself in Pall Mall, with sore feet which had been trodden on many times. A soldier, just a little drunk, was on the pedestal of Florence Nightingale's statue, with his arm around the figure of that lady. He was making a speech to which no one listened except myself. Over and over again he assured the crowds that the bloody war wouldn't have been won without the help of women like good old Florence. "It's the women of

England who won the war," he shouted, "and that's the bloody truth of it!" No one challenged this statement.

No one listened except me, curious to know what he was saying with such fervour and passion. I never pass the statue of Florence Nightingale now without thinking of that champion of womanhood who was a little drunk.

After the Victory March, what then? — There had been riots among the men even on the parade ground of Whitehall because of delay in demobilisation. They had done their bit. They were fed up with Army discipline. They wanted to fling off their uniforms and get back to Civvy Street. Millions of them did before long, but Civvy Street was not strewn with roses nor paved with gold. It was difficult to find jobs. Women had taken many of the places for lower wages than men and employers were loth to let them go.

Employers in city offices received the personal applications of young officers somewhat coldly. "What do you know?" they asked of young men who had left their public schools to join the New Armies, who had been very fine machine-gunners, or pilots of aircraft, or tank officers, or with the P.B.I. which was the "Poor Bloody Infantry". Many of them had been captains and majors before the age of twenty-five. But they couldn't answer that question: "What do you know?" very satisfactorily. They had had no training in office work. They had not been trained for anything except war, which was now at an end. Some of them bought little farms and lost their money. Some of them went in for chickens, and lost their money. Some of them became agents for vacuum cleaners, or cosmetics, or women's underwear, and hated ringing the door bells to ask for the lady of the house, and could not make a go of it.

So it was with the men during this transition from war to peace and afterwards — for years afterwards — during the tides of unemployment. . . .

28 Read the following extract carefully then summarise its contents in no more than 150 words. State at the end the number you have used.

Japan is an industrial country dominated by small workshops rather than large factories. Its industrial structure makes it very difficult indeed for local and central government to control environmental damage. By 1967 there were 83,820 factories in Tokyo alone and 70 per cent of them had ten employees or less. Two Tokyo wards accommodated 600 factories per square kilometre. Workshops are often embedded within the residential and commercial areas and their owners have scant reserves for financing anti-pollution measures. The flimsy construction of many workshops is partly responsible for the severe noise problem in Japanese cities. In the whole of Japan in 1969 there were almost 650,000 industrial enterprises and the table below gives some indication of their size and importance, as measured by employment.

Industrial enterprises in Japan 1969

Number of employees by industrial enterprise	Number of establishments	Percentage of establishments	Percentage of workforce
under 10	475,058	73.4	16.6
10-99	156,597	24.2	35.6
100-999	14,393	2.2	30.4
1000 and over	878	0.2	17.4

The problem of controlling so many enterprises would be difficult for a country with an effective body of legislation regarding pollution and the necessary will to enforce it, with a modest economic growth rate, with stable firms and with powers for regulating the use of land. None of these conditions exist in Japan. The Western visitor is immediately struck by the absence of zoning and by the "indiscriminate scatter" of homes and factories. Although more rigorous control of land use is now being attempted, the recent lack of effective zoning laws to separate functions has resulted in chaos.

Moreover, the unceasing urban and industrial pressure has spilled over from the main centres into contiguous areas. Even in these "new" areas the opportunity to exercise some control over land-use for development has not been taken. During the past two decades of unusually rapid industrial growth, both zoning and anti-pollution regulations have been far too weak to deal effectively with the tremendous pressures unleashed — for land, for water, for air, for effluent disposal, for transport systems and so on — by the multitude of busy Japanese entrepreneurs.

29   This extract is taken from a science fiction novel called *The Drought*. Write a summary in three paragraphs covering

a) the gradual spread of drought conditions during the ten years previous to the extract; b) the real cause of the world-wide drought; c) attempts to beat the drought and why they failed. Your whole summary should not exceed 150 words. State at the end the number used.

The world-wide drought now in its fifth month was the culmination of a series of extended droughts that had taken place with increasing frequency all over the globe during the previous decade. Ten years earlier a critical shortage of world food-stuffs had occurred when the seasonal rainfall expected in a number of important agricultural areas had failed to materialize. One by one, areas as far apart as Saskatchewan and the Loire valley, Kazakhstan and the Madras tea country were turned into arid dust-basins. The following months brought little more than a few inches of rain, and after two years these farmlands were totally devastated. Once their populations had resettled themselves elsewhere, these new deserts were abandoned for good.

The continued appearance of more and more such areas on the map, and the added difficulties of making good the world's food supplies, led to the first attempts at some form of global weather control. A survey by the U.N. Food and Agriculture Organization showed that everywhere river levels and water tables were falling. The two-and-a-half million square miles drained by the Amazon had shrunk to less than half this area. Scores of its tributaries had dried up completely, and aerial surveys discovered that much of the former rain-forest was already dry and petrified. At Khartoum, in lower Egypt, the White Nile was twenty feet below its mean level ten years earlier, and lower outlets were bored in the concrete barrage of the dam at Aswan.

Despite world-wide attempts at cloud-seeding, the amounts of rainfall continued to diminish. The seeding operations finally ended when it was obvious that not only was there no rain, but there were no clouds. At this point attention switched to the ultimate source of rainfall — the ocean surface. It needed only the briefest scientific examination to show that here were the origins of the drought.

Covering the off-shore waters of the world's oceans, to a distance of about a thousand miles from the coast, was a thin but resilient mono-molecular film formed from a complex of saturated long-chain polymers, generated within the sea from the vast quantities of industrial wastes discharged into the

ocean basins during the previous fifty years. This tough,
oxygen-permeable membrane lay on the air-water interface
and prevented almost all evaporation of surface water into
the air space above. Although the structure of these polymers
was quickly identified, no means was found of removing
them. The saturated linkages produced in the perfect organic
bath of the sea were completely non-reactive, and formed an
intact seal broken only when the water was violently disturbed.
Fleets of trawlers and naval craft equipped with rotating
flails began to ply up and down the Atlantic and Pacific
coasts of North America, and along the sea-boards of Western
Europe, but without any long-term effects. Likewise the
removal of the entire surface water provided only a temporary
respite — the film quickly replaced itself by lateral extension
from the surrounding surface, recharged by precipitation
from the reservoir below.

30 Write a summary of the following passage in good continuous prose, using no more than 150 words. State at the end the
number used. The passage contains 511 words.

There are times when it seems as though we are drowning in a
welter of horror stories about comprehensive schools. Exactly
why society has this compulsive need to turn on its prisons,
mental hospitals, old people's homes and schools in this way,
making them into the subjects of press exposures and lurid
television documentaries, is not clear — the psychologists
would probably find evidence of guilt sublimation — but it is a
habit which makes all manner of difficulties for the people
who have to work in them. The very latest crop of tales runs
pretty true to form; a retired selective girls' school head-
mistress goes to teach in a comprehensive and has to pack it
in within a week. The *Sunday Times* prints an impassioned
piece from a young teacher who has had a chair thrown at
her; the following week there is a letter from a lady who
quelled a riot in class by felling the ringleaders with one blow
of her fist — she is unsure whether or not to feel guilty about
this, but confesses to have gained by carrying such a
reputation, rather like that fairy tale character who had
"Seven At One Blow" inscribed on a placard hanging on his
person.
    Exactly what members of the public at large think when
they read these tales I do not know, but they can hardly, to
say the least, be reassured. The stage is being reached where
everyone firmly believes that our schools have become places

of continuing anarchy and violence; where teachers go about shielding their heads from falling chairs and flying dustbin lids, and where a black belt in Aikido is of greater pedagogic relevance than the Licentiate of the College of Preceptors.

Part of the trouble is in the poor public relations performance of most schools, which makes them easy prey to the media man who is looking for something exciting, and which ensures that the only time the surrounding neighbourhood hears about them is when something goes bang. It is true, I think, that tales of malevolent conduct are seized upon hungrily by press and public alike. Partly, of course, what we have here is the old "man bites dog" dilemma which besets the newspapers. The fact that children are working hard and behaving themselves is not nearly so attractive to hear as is the news that they are burning their classrooms and tarring and feathering their unfortunate teachers. Can you, after all, imagine a news story like this?

PEACE AND QUIET IN COVENTRY SCHOOL

Forty children sat quietly today in Calford Comprehensive while their teacher, overweight, balding Jimmy Smith (46) told them about the causes of the English Civil War.

Trousers

The boys were all dressed in grey trousers. Several were wearing school ties.

Feeling

Interviewed later, Mr Smith said, "I have a feeling that we are getting to the essence of what the Civil War is all about." A number of the children wrote details of the war in their exercise books, and one or two of them openly intended to do some homework.

31 All the following statements were made during a debate on the motion that "The United Kingdom should come into line with the rest of Europe and drive on the right." Using only the opinions presented here and ignoring any that you think are irrelevant, summarise in clear and correct English a) the case *for* the UK driving on the right (max. words 80) and b) the case *against* (max. words 100).

    1 Most of the countries in the world drive on the right: so should the U.K.

2 The cost of converting road signs, road markings etc. would be enormous.
3 Cars are no longer a luxury: they are an essential part of modern life.
4 All buses and coaches would have to be converted to right hand loading.
5 The UK is adopting the metric system: driving on the right is a logical extension of this.
6 More heavy traffic should be diverted to the railways.
7 All existing vehicles would have to be changed over to left hand drive, at enormous expense. Who would pay?
8 Driving on the right would help foreign motorists on business or pleasure in Britain; the accident rate would drop.
9 The Highway Code would have to be re-written and all road safety habits re-learned.
10 The UK is surrounded by water. There is no problem of drivers having to switch to the other side of the road at a land frontier.
11 Heavy lorries are already pounding British roads to pieces.
12 Sweden successfully changed from driving on the left to driving on the right.
13 The accident rate would shoot up if a change-over was made — particularly among the old and the young.
14 Why should Britain copy the Continent? We should continue to assert our independence.
15 Manufacturing only left hand drive cars would help the British motor industry. Exports would be easier.
16 An immense and costly programme of driver education would be needed.
17 The tax on petrol should be devoted exclusively to road maintenance and building.
18 Great Britain has joined the European Economic Community: it should adopt their way of driving.
19 All one-way traffic systems in Britain would have to be re-designed.
20 Continental drivers have coped in the UK in the past: they can continue to do so.
21 Driving at home on the right would help British drivers when they go abroad.
22 The United Kingdom could not afford the change: it is going through a period of financial restraint.
23 A referendum should be held before any decision is made.

32 Write a summary of the following passage in good continuous prose, using no more than 150 words. State at the end the number used. The passage contains 456 words.

What has gone wrong with young people today? They are undisciplined, assertive, selfish and lacking all the restraints hitherto associated with the formative years. One does not look for a return to the Victorian era when "Children should be seen but not heard" was the order of the day but surely the pendulum has swung to the other extreme and a swing back is due before our eardrums burst.

Why should children, whose experience is so limited, be allowed to dominate so many homes? It is perhaps natural that they should monopolize the stage in the early years of infancy but one would expect them to see less of the limelight as they begin their formal education at the age of five or thereabouts. Instead of being put more and more firmly in their place, however, they are encouraged by consenting adults to bigger and better orgies of self-expression. "What would you like for tea, darling?" "Do you want to read this morning, dear, or would you prefer to play with the sand?" "It's rather naughty to knock Darren over but I expect you didn't mean it." Is it surprising, after years of this sort of indoctrination, that the national motto of our youth when asked to do something seems to be "Why should I?"

The current craze for self-expression ought to be replaced by a good stiff dose of repression. Why do youngsters have to blazen their names all over walls and railway carriages? Does the rest of the world really care that "Liz was 'ere"? Is she — and Dave and Trev and Mick — so self-centred that she can't see the visual mess she is making of the environment we all share?

Another source of irritation is the constant stream of pop music from blaring transistors. Some teenagers even seem unable in their more serious moments to study or "concentrate" without a background of noise punctuated by inane remarks. It is sad to see that the rising generation of a once great nation has fallen so low as to be obsessed with trivia.

Of course one realizes that not every youngster indulges in football punch-ups, in loud-mouthed obscenities, in vacuous graffiti. There are thousands participating in the Duke of Edinburgh's Award Scheme, in social service projects of all kinds, in the numerous youth organizations. But, to use the concept of the moment, the "image" of the adolescent has never been so tarnished. And in a world that judges increasingly by appearances, it is up to the silent majority of young people to restrain the exhibitionist minority from so flagrantly drawing attention to themselves as a means of compensating for their own inadequacy. If they don't, the pendulum may rock so violently that the clock will have to be put back a hundred years.

Index of Authors and Titles